Student of the Game

Navigating the video game industry is like playing on expert mode – without a strategy guide.

In this rapidly evolving, hit-driven industry, technology advances at breakneck speed while personalities and business dynamics shift constantly. Many aspiring professionals ask how to break into game audio, but fewer discuss what happens after you're in – or how to avoid getting lost along the way.

Student of the Game offers a rare, unfiltered perspective from an independent video game composer who has survived and thrived over the past decade. Through candid anecdotes and hard-won insights, this book reveals:

- *The reality behind industry buzzwords* like "networking" and "imposter syndrome"
- *Practical strategies for building sustainable professional relationships*
- *Red flags and pitfalls* that can derail promising collaborations
- *Mental frameworks for persistence* when facing inevitable setbacks
- *The truth about gigs that didn't work out* – and why

This isn't just another "how to break in" guide. It's a survival manual for anyone serious about building a lasting career in game audio, complete with the aches, breaks and breakthroughs that define professional growth in this challenging but rewarding field.

Chase Bethea is a multi-award-winning video game composer known as the "Swiss army knife of video game composition." His acclaimed scores include *I Can't Escape: Darkness*, *Aground* and *On the Peril of Parrots*. Chase has made history multiple times, including being the first video game composer on the Mogami Cable roster and being featured in books such as *Global Histories of Video Game Music Technology* and *The Theory and Practice of Writing Music for Games*. He has delivered 60+ talks at GDC, PAX, Berklee and more.

Student of the Game

Navigating a Decade in the Video Game Industry

Chase Bethea

CRC Press
Taylor & Francis Group
Boca Raton London New York

CRC Press is an imprint of the
Taylor & Francis Group, an **informa** business

Designed cover image: Chase Bethea

First edition published 2027
by CRC Press
2385 NW Executive Center Drive, Suite 320, Boca Raton FL 33431

and by CRC Press
4 Park Square, Milton Park, Abingdon, Oxon, OX14 4RN

CRC Press is an imprint of Taylor & Francis Group, LLC

ISBN: 978-1-032-72832-2 (hbk)
ISBN: 978-1-032-68539-7 (pbk)
ISBN: 978-1-003-42281-5 (ebk)

DOI: 10.1201/9781003422815

Typeset in Minion
by Apex CoVantage, LLC

Contents

Preface

My goal is not to heavily criticise, be rude, nor do I seek sympathy. My goal is to simply share my insights that I have heard from others in the industry space I have been in. In addition, guide the reader through my thought process on how to come out the other side with a better perspective in order to continue to persevere and be successful. Please try not to take what I say personally as these are my specific experiences and perspectives on how I approach solutions.

As you will notice, throughout this book, I will be very careful in my choice of words, when talking about certain circumstances, anecdotes and experiences. Therefore, when you see words, such as "normally, usually, often, sometimes, occasionally, rarely," I am trying to gauge as best as I can from my experience. Often, I have found that these experiences have occurred in other people's lives too. I feel this is important because it is my guess that most people who are reading this book are trying to get perspective on what is common in the industry, especially those who are newcomers.

About the Author

Chase Bethea is a multi-award-winning video game composer known in the industry as the "Swiss army knife of video game composition." With over a decade of experience, Chase's music has enhanced the player's experience across a diverse range of games. His work is celebrated for its unique fusion of orchestral, electronic and world music elements and has been performed by ensembles like the Helix Collective, New York Gamer Symphony and other orchestras worldwide. His soundtrack for *Cubic Climber* earned a Noteworthy on Destructoid. Notable projects include the critically acclaimed soundtracks for *I Can't Escape: Darkness* (nominated for Artist of the Year), *Aground* (NYX Award for Best Original Soundtrack), *Aground Zero* (NYX Award Gold and International Architecture & Design Platinum Award for Best Original Soundtrack) and *On the Peril of Parrots*, which garnered two Global Music Awards, one for the same score and the other recognising Chase's excellence as a composer. In March 2024, Chase was honoured with one of the industry's most prestigious awards: the "Excellence in Artistry" Award from the Black in Gaming Foundation. This recognition serves as a testament to his consistent dedication and remarkable contributions to video game music within the industry.

Chase is also a dynamic guest speaker and live performer, showcasing his talents at prestigious game conferences such as MAGWest/MAGFest. Over the past several years, he has given more than 60 talks at conferences, colleges, universities and institutions, including as a keynote speaker at Global Game Jam, Game Developer's Conference (GDC), Penny Arcade Expo (PAX), Berklee College of Music, Game Devs of Colour, Gamesound Con, Audio Developers Conference (ADC), American Association of

Independent Music (A2IM), International Game Developers Association (IGDA) BIGFest, Xsolla, Pocket Gamer and Mobile Growth Summit (MGS) at The Strat in Las Vegas. His contributions to the industry have been recognised with exhibitions in the NAMM Museum and the British Library, and he has shared his insights through articles published in multiple global magazines and books such as *Recording Magazine*, *Fearzine*, *ROM*, *Sweetwater*, *GB Studio*, *Global Histories of Video Game Music Technology*, *The Theory and Practice of Writing Music for Games* and *Ludic Narrans*. Chase was also the Interactive Special Interest Group (iASIG) Steering Committee Chairman (2022–2024).

In 2024, Chase made more history as the first video game composer to join the prestigious Mogami Cable roster, further solidifying his impact on the industry. As a video game composer, Chase has brought his special signature sound to big libraries and has worked with and written demos for Spitfire, Reason Studios and Soundiron, curated selections for Native Instruments Sounds.com and added to the artist roster of the legendary ILIO and Q Up Arts. Chase has also collaborated with Shure Microphones and Mojave Audio.

Chase's passion for innovation in game music continues as he solidifies his reputation as a leading voice in the industry.

CHAPTER 1

Story Mode

1.1 [LEVEL 1 – FIRST STAGE]

1.1.1 How Did I Get Started

I was born and raised in Chicago until I was 13. I was in the advanced band and choir from fifth–seventh grade. From fifth grade, during my saxophone practice at home, I started composing melodies out of boredom from the music pieces I was learning. I would listen to WNUA 95.5 (a smooth jazz station that used to air in Chicago) and would transcribe my favourite songs on normal paper by ear from the radio. My father did not know about manuscript paper and neither did I. So, although I read sheet music, I could not write the notes. I could only write the letters of the notes. In addition, melodies were coming to me often because I was singing regularly and making remixes of cartoon songs in my head.

Another composing process that I started a year before was making music on Game Boy Camera. I suppose this is where and when I started writing game music. There is a section of the game, where you navigate to a mini game where you pretend to be a DJ. You start off by pressing the start button and then you are taken to another screen where you can create a rhythm on a noise channel, design different waveforms and select notes.

1.2 [LEVEL 2 – SECOND STAGE]

I moved to Los Angeles, California in 2001. I primarily lived between Sherman Oaks and Simi Valley. Later on in secondary school, I was making music on the computer using software like Hammertime and Fruity

DOI: 10.1201/9781003422815-1

FIGURE 1.1 Composing on Game Boy Camera

Loops 3. I recall making my first music track on my Pentium 2 Dell Computer, burning it to a CD, walking to the bus stop and showing the track to this girl named Tasha. "Hey, Tasha", I said, "Do you want to hear a track I made?" "Sure", she said. She took the headphones from my hands, put them on and listened. She did not show much expression while listening. Tasha proceeded to take off the headphones and handed them back to me. "It's cool but it sounds like it should be in a video game," she said. From that point forward, no matter how many tracks I made, people told me it sounded like video game music. I took it as an insult because I wanted to make Hip-Hop. I never could escape the video game music sound I was told that I had. However, what I did not know and later realised is that my signature sound was established very early.

1.3 [LEVEL 3 – THIRD STAGE]

A year before graduating, I knew that I wanted to attend the Los Angeles Recording School to hone my audio production skills. So, I enrolled in that school the same year I graduated High School (2006–2007). If only I had a more optimistic mind and I regret this still, I would have listened to the people who told me my music sounds like video game music and would have figured out how to pursue it sooner.

I realised in 2008 that I wanted to work in the video game field. The hint had always been thrown at me subtly, but it never clicked until I was working at an internet media company called Music Plus Television and later to be rebranded as Vlaze. I had composed some orchestral music for a video clip, and my friend, Jason, who worked there as the main IT guy, told me that it sounded similar to *Castle Crashers*. From there, I researched the game and compared the music. Then, I realised I could do this. At that point, I began to pursue my career in video games.

1.3.1 [Demo Stage]

When I finally decided to listen to people saying that my music sounded like it should be in a video game, I did an implementation test. I found this 2D fighting game engine called M.U.G.E.N. This was a freeware, customisable fighting game engine where you could have the Death Star fight Sephrioth or Homer Simpson fight Yusuke Urameshi (a character from the Anime "Yu Yu Hakusho"). You could customise your character select screen and fighting level background as well as sound effect for your character and music per fighting level. So, I took a music piece that I composed and coded it in. Since I had learned HTML code in high school and won best website design based on that code, editing code in M.U.G.E.N. was easy to follow and do. Once I heard my music in the game, it all made sense. I was hooked. I proceeded to add more of my music to the M.U.G.E.N.

FIGURE 1.2 M.U.G.E.N.

engine. It completely blew my mind that my music was playing while some of my work colleagues were fighting with their favourite characters. From that point on, it wasn't enough, I needed more.

So, I decided to return to school to bridge the gap with any music knowledge I lacked as I knew I would be competing against the AAA composers.

1.4 [LEVEL 4 – FOURTH STAGE]

My years in attendance at Moorpark College were the best time. Here was where I began my composition journey to become a video game composer. During this period, I was playing catch-up as well as reinventing myself. I was taking classical piano and made it into their elite applied music program. Orbie Ingersoll (Music Professor), Professor James Song (Former Department Chair/Symphony Orchestra Conductor), Mona DeCesare (Pianist) and Sheila Rumenapp (Math Teacher) were my most beloved professors, and I am so thankful for them.

During my final music theory class at Moorpark College, I knew I could not wait until I graduated to start working in the industry. I had a part-time job at LensCrafters and a co-worker had an uncle that was working in games. His uncle introduced me to the CEO of the mobile game studio,

FIGURE 1.3 Professor James Song and Chase Bethea

and I was able to obtain a paid internship (Mobotory - 2011). Less than a year later, the studio shut down, and I did some research on how to be a freelancer in game audio. I found the book, *The Complete Guide to Game Audio* by Aaron Marks.

I read half of the book and applied to two music requests on a game developer forum. I received a bite from one, wrote a one-minute music demo and got the gig. The game project turned out to be paid and it shipped in six months. The mobile game is called *Electron Flux* (2012).

By now, you can see that my path was somewhat unorthodox. Stories that I normally have heard after being in the industry for five years was the receiving of mentorship. However, I discovered how to ship my first game on my own. I believe this achievement came from learning and tinkering with M.U.G.E.N. and then by the combination of reading the book, *A Complete Guide to Game Audio*, before I even went to any game conference.

In 2016, I transferred to CSUN (California State University, Northridge) with the intent to strengthen my orchestration skills and learn video game composition. By this time, I had already been in the industry for four years, shipped several games and was nominated in the industry via

FIGURE 1.4 The Package Deal to My Success

VGMO (Video Game Music Online) for Best Artist of the Year. While at CSUN, I was told that there was not a video game class for composition. For the first semester that I was there, the university did not have a video game club. In the same semester, I did some research in the computer science department, emailing teachers, through the school's directory until I stumbled upon the art department. They started a video game club the following semester. I joined the club immediately and became the first game audio composer within the club. I also participated in the first inaugural game club game jam. I quickly became the liaison and made introductions for peers in my music composition program to collaborate with other game developers who wanted to work on games.

1.5 [LEVEL 5 – FIFTH STAGE]

Well, this is where the book begins.

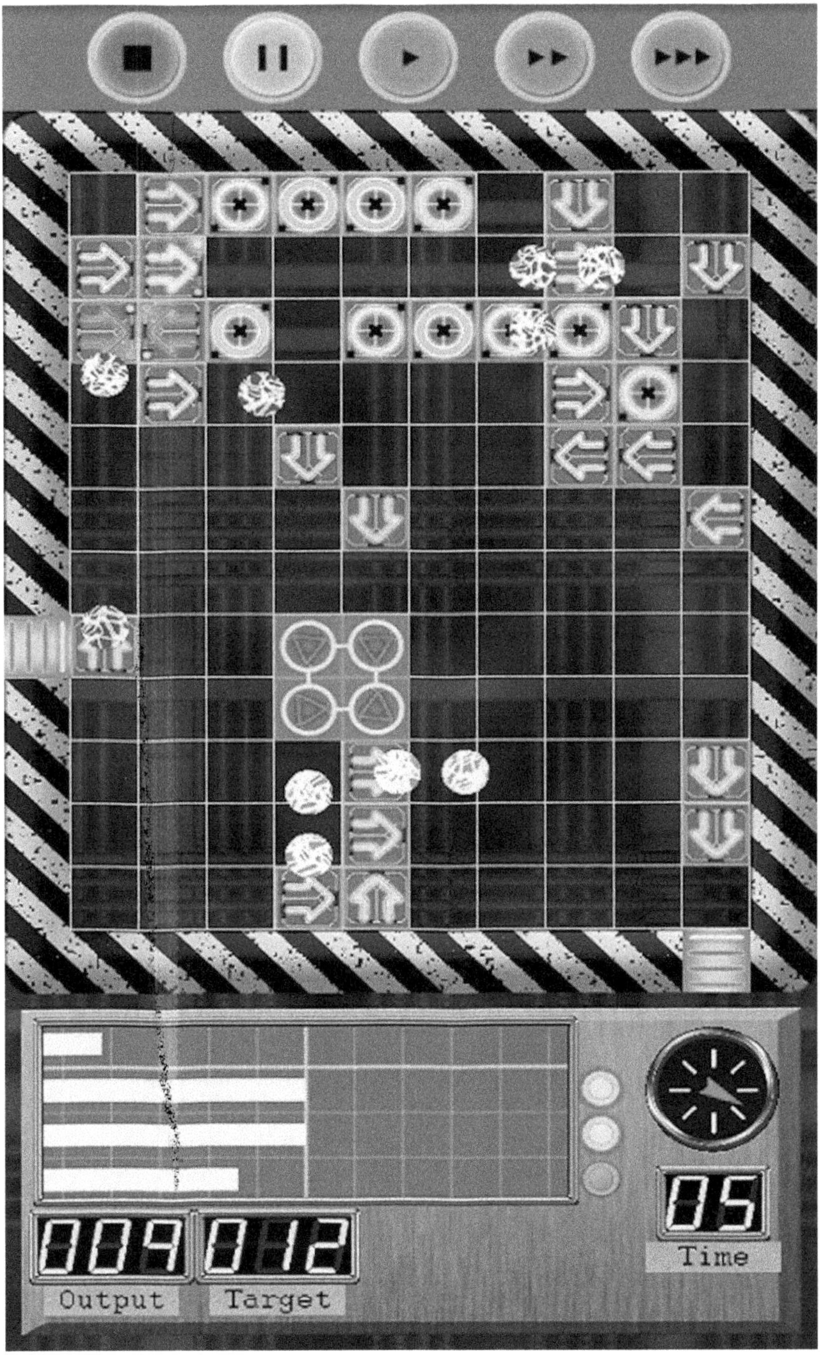

FIGURE 1.5 *Electron Flux* Gameplay

FIGURE 1.6 Chase Bethea Timeline-1

FIGURE 1.7 Chase Bethea Timeline-2

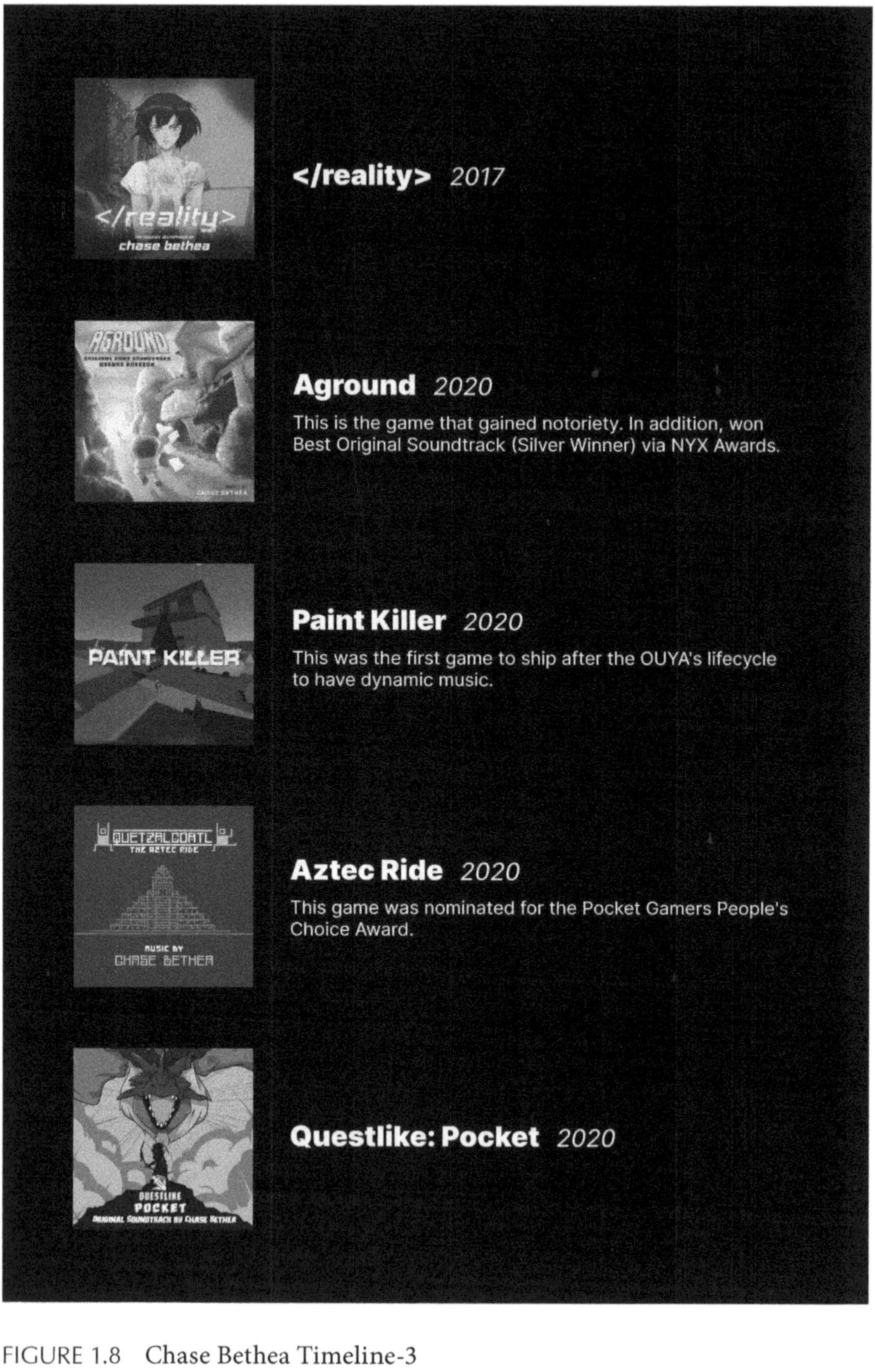

FIGURE 1.8 Chase Bethea Timeline-3

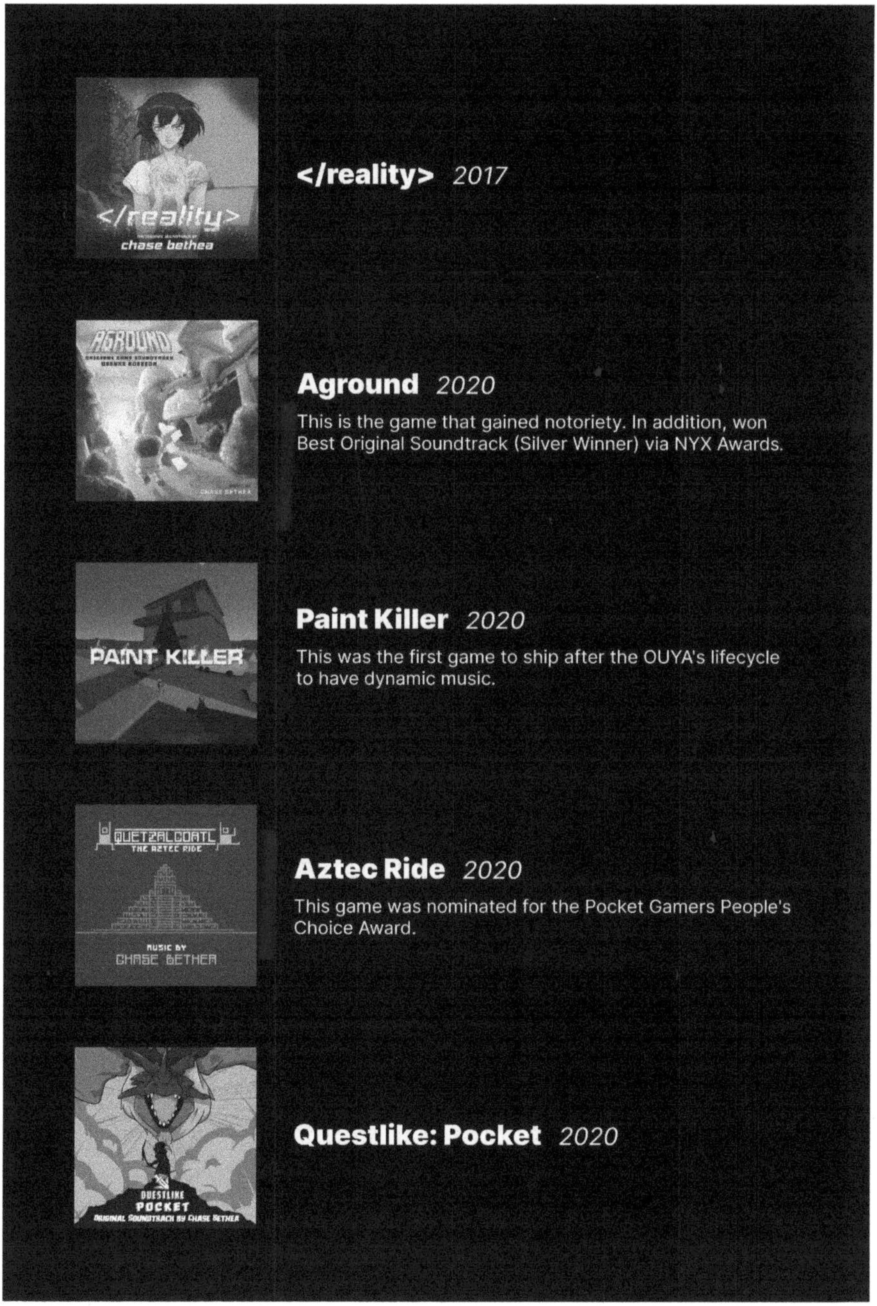

FIGURE 1.8 Chase Bethea Timeline-3

FIGURE 1.7 Chase Bethea Timeline-2

CHAPTER 2

Starting Points/ Stat Distribution

Harness the power of patience. If you do that, you'll always be where you are supposed to be and happy about it. I learned this lesson when I started to play *Dark Souls* for the first time in 2020. It did not occur to me that whenever you encounter a boss and they are hard to beat, that games have been designing and implementing this level of difficulty and challenge for a long time. There is some kind of player conditioning that when we play the game, we want to try to hurry up and finish it by beating up as many enemies as we can, doing combos and rushing through enemies. It gives us a false perception that once we reach the boss, we are able to handle those smaller enemies the same way with the same vigour by just attacking fast. However, in my opinion, this is not a good mental approach to how you should defeat the boss. You have to go into the boss battle with patience. You have to understand the boss' movement patterns, counter-attacks and anything else it throws at you. This is why it takes so long to beat a boss but if you do not go into the battle with patience eventually, you may become frustrated. You may possibly believe that you are not able to beat the boss. So, what I have learned is that going in with patience and knowing that the boss will not be beaten swiftly, but that there is an art to taking your time. There is a dance to be had with the boss, and it may take 30 minutes to an hour or more to defeat. The boss fight is really where the patience metre is built.

DOI: 10.1201/9781003422815-2

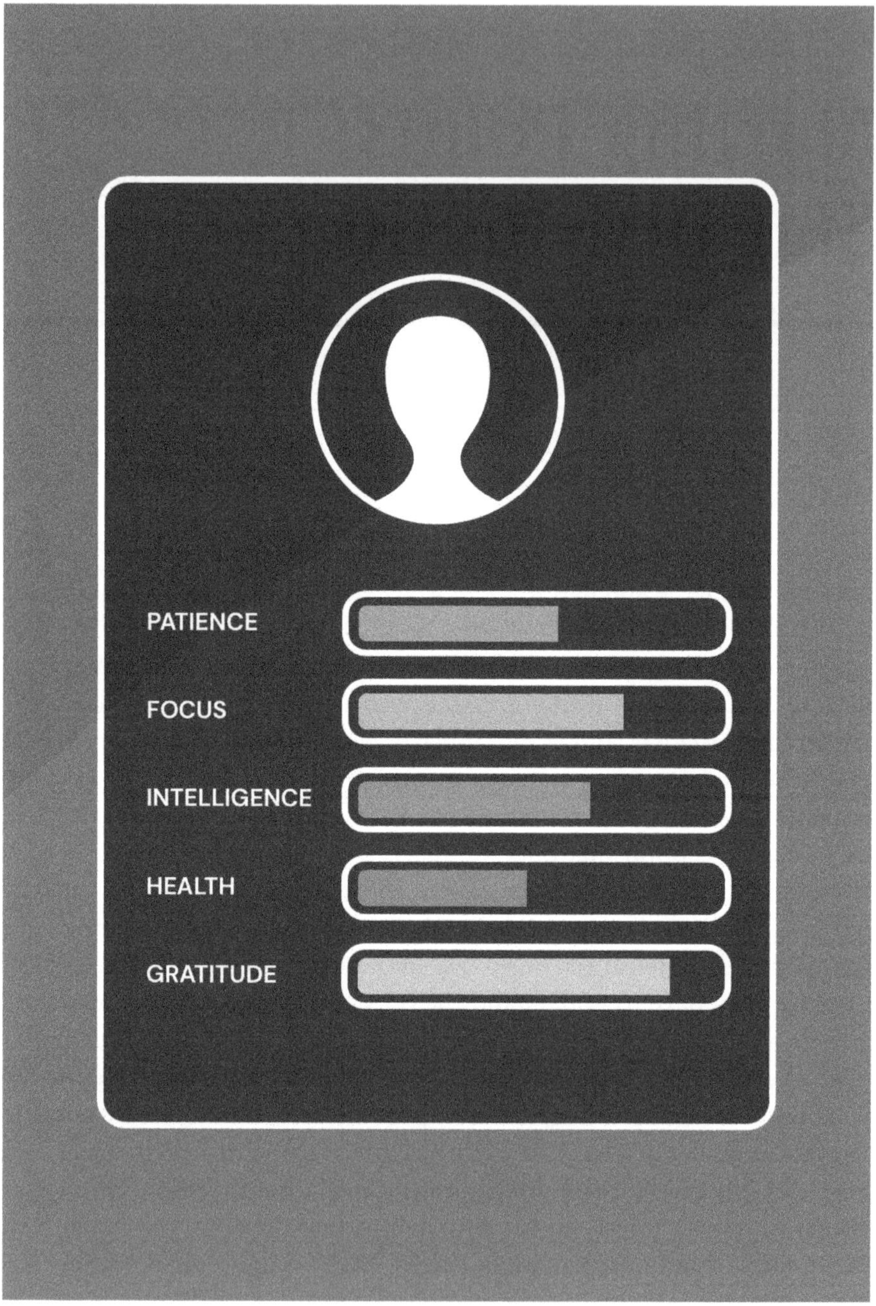

FIGURE 2.1 Stats that Relate to the Career

This applies to the industry. The tech and games industry changes rapidly and sometimes some people's careers do too. However, when that moment in life comes when you are frustrated, look at it as the boss fight that irked you and apply that patience mentally. You will overcome the frustration just as you did with those tough-to-beat bosses. You will prevail.

You should not be concerned with who is ahead of you. Focus hard on where you are and grow accordingly. A lot of industry colleagues, acquaintances and some friends surpassed me in their career but when I started getting recognised for some of my work, those same people that were ahead of me looked back to see where I was. Maybe they thought I was catching up to them. Who knows? However, I continued to look and move forward. I kept on doing my own thing.

The benefit of having two financial advisors and many lawyers (one on almost every continent. I'm looking for one in Antarctica). I chose people who live their life so naturally. These people are also not readily available but that does not mean my life should stop for them too. I have to keep going and pivoting. So being able to have multiple contacts gives me the option to reach out to one and then another if the first contact is too busy. It can also benefit to receive perspectives from each contact and opinions to mix and match.

Daily workouts levelled me up spiritually as well as physically. Every day, I levelled up my mind, body and heart. With these workouts, it opened my mind with clarity and creativity. There were mental "problem walls" that I was running into that got resolved during workouts. These exercises consisted of cardio, high intensity hits, weights and various other exercises and allowed ideas and solutions to flow naturally. I felt I was building my body and my mind together and with that my heart became fuller. Full of gratitude and appreciation. I slowly became happier and healthier and creatively it showed in my work, my work ethic and other content I produced.

My goal when I began the workouts was to train myself to run a marathon. I figured the industry is a marathon. So, if I could physically relate it to that, I could succeed and sustain in this industry more successfully into the next decade. I'm still training and building strength, and as I surpass my decade milestone into the next one, I continue to build upon the work I have put in and the results have become more mirific on a monthly basis.

CHAPTER 3

Inventory

Over the 30 podcast interviews I have done in the past decade, many people inquire about my creative process. This changes over time as projects evolve and I mature with my creativity. Most importantly, it is all about figuring out what fits the game best. I think about choosing my instruments for audio consistency, using various techniques and tools to create what is in my head for the game and test it. Viewing my work from the perspective of the player is important. I play games and listen well. I know what would and would not annoy me as a player. I try my best to avoid those annoyances and instead convey positive and effective sounds and tunes for the game. In all, I want to make ear candy for the player.

A composer is a masterful translator of emotion that uses musical notes to build textures and integrate into the project as well as being a piece of glue of the entire art form for people to experience.

My sound has always been unique. Unique unfortunately does not catch on to people right away. What I have noticed though is that it is my sound that is recognisable and becomes appreciated over time. It grows on you for a lifetime.

In the book, *What to Listen For* by Aaron Copland, he touches on so many things I have had quarries with when people give me their, solicited and unsolicited, opinions about my music.

Here are some quotes that resonated with me when I began reading it on September 10, 2021:

> There is, however, such a thing as becoming more sensitive to different kinds of sound stuff as used by various composers. For all

DOI: 10.1201/9781003422815-3

> composers do not use that sound stuff in the same way. Don't get the idea that the value of music is commensurate with its sensuous appeal or that the loveliest sounding music is made by the greatest composer. If that were so, Ravel would be a greater creator than Beethoven. The point is that the sound element varies with each composer, that the usage of sound forms an integral part of his style and must be taken into account when listening. (Page 11)

Many times, I have been compared to no one. So, because I am not "box worthy" (meaning no one can put me in a box), I get pushed aside. Copland talks about not just listening but listening for something. Ironically, I have always written my music to be something people can dive deeper into. "Not just listening but listening for something." Yet, it is never measured, and people do not realise until later that things are dull. All the while, I was writing because I foresaw those dull periods approaching or was already in it. I took the mantra from a Mad Men quote, "If you don't like what's being said, then change the conversation." I spun that to be, "If you don't like

FIGURE 3.1 Inditing

what's being played, write something different." Different doesn't always make you popular or get you recognition. However, differences do keep things moving forward, refreshing, new, exciting and sometimes memorable. So, when I start the creative process, these are a few things I think of.

1. Come up with a name. A list of names I have written down. Choose one. This is so I don't have to change the name of the Digital Audio Workstation (DAW) session later. If I don't, then this can be a pain in the ass.
2. Name the file in the DAW.
3. Build the sound palette or edit the sound palette.
4. Play the game, read the game design doc and hear what the game is asking for.
5. Come up with a "word" theme, i.e., Boss, "aggression", "space", "magic", "relaxing".
6. Design rhythms, chord textures and multiple melodies to match the "word theme".
7. Try to write at least four bars.
8. Every bar counts as a format because it could be a section for the dynamic music stem.
9. Mark each section.
10. Send a draft, or once finished writing the minutes, for approval to the client.
11. Once approved, check the mix on different systems (Cell phone/ headphones. Car is the best).
12. Render out each section and/or create loops.
13. Render the full arrangement.
14. Render stems of full arrangement.
15. Clean up the session – unused tracks, synths, recorded files, etc.
16. Upload the files to the repository or send files.

17. Dynamic music steps – implement the music.
18. Edit code and/or software to fit seamlessly with the game mechanics (i.e. If the music changes between combat and exploration or items, the fades have to be edited in code or software to achieve it).
19. Update the audio asset sheet with progress, bpm, key, tempo, length and genre tags.
20. Master the track.
21. Make different track versions (MP3/WAV).
22. Update the metadata/ISRC.
23. Register the music with my PRO and SoundExchange.

I have found that this process has been the most streamlined. Somewhere between steps five and six, I may record live instruments for the score or hire a musician to record something I cannot play. In some cases, I may hire an orchestra as well but only if there is a budget for it and the game calls for it too.

Staying creative is one of the most challenging things being an artist musician. When I was a baby, I had a wooden toy chest, and it had all my toys in it. I wanted to recreate that in physical form for instruments. There is something about connecting with the instrument in your hand versus the virtual instruments. Virtual instruments (VSTs) are great because they give access to instruments you would not otherwise have physically and are professionally recorded. However, the feeling of string plucking or striking keys and adjusting reeds is unmeasured.

I used to watch the anime, "Bleach" and I was impacted deeply by Ichigo connecting with his "Zanpakuto" and one of his spirits within that he acknowledged as "Old man Zangetsu". The sword had life, and when he connected with his Zanpakuto, he became stronger. I applied this ideology to the piano, and when I did, I noticed a major difference in my playing. I felt as if the piano were synchronised. Since I moved places a lot, I knew that I unfortunately would not be able to move my piano with me, so I recreated my toy chest but with instruments that I have collected from

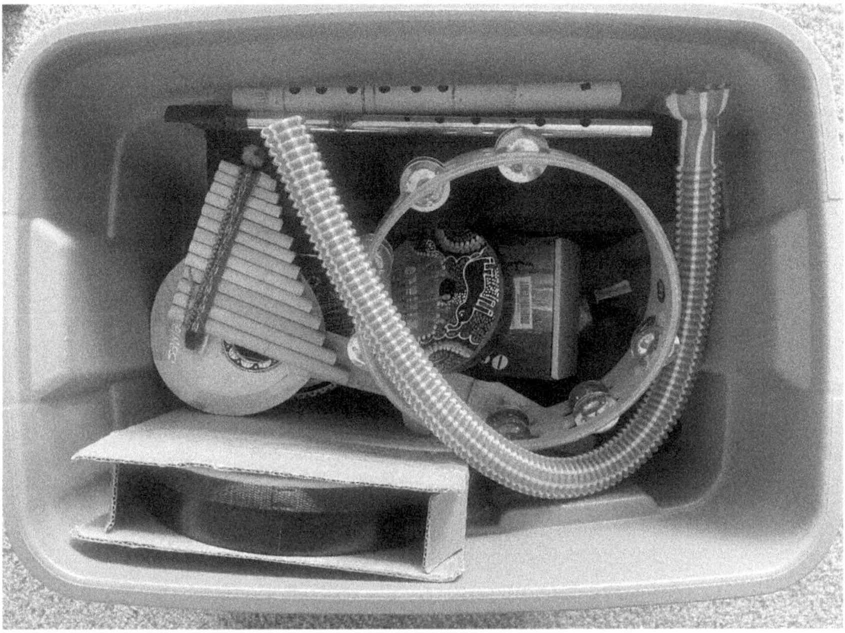

FIGURE 3.2 Instrument Toy Chest

FIGURE 3.3 Instrument Toys

places I have visited in the world, gifts from friends as well as the few that my Mum bought me when I was a child.

Windfish flutes, Maracas, Native Flutes, Harmonicas, Coconut Kalimbas, Whirly tubes, Jaw Harps, Tiny Tongue Drums, Hand Drums, Ocarinas and more. This "toy chest collection" is my inventory, and between that and the VSTs, the curiosity keeps me creative.

CHAPTER 4

Putting Your Own Spin on It

What does this mean? It took me years to figure out what this really meant. What I have discovered is that when you want to put your own spin on it, it means these three things.

Number one is using your imagination. As children, we have an abundance of this. Somewhere along the way of growing into an adult, we lose it more and more as responsibilities take over the focus. Sometimes, the imagination gets redirected depending on how full our day is, where we can have a hobby or two to use or if we work in a creative space where we use it in our daily work. However, for me to have this imagination be at its maximum, a lot of things need to be cleared off my plate and taken care of. Bills and rent are paid on time, income is stable and little to no drama in my personal life. Once those things align, I noticed that I do not have to think so hard and my mind wanders freely like it used to when I was a child. So, how can I maintain this imagination maximum? The truth is I cannot but when my imagination spurts occur, I take full advantage. I do a brain dump and scribe every idea that comes to me so that I am able to utilise it later to avoid or pivot away from any future creative blocks.

Number two is experimenting. This is another childhood characteristic. Staying curious and doing experiments to obtain knowledge and experience. It is the raw experience we have as children that thrives. When we experiment, this is where some of the magic happens. "What if . . ." and the process goes wild from there. We are taught about this action in school,

DOI: 10.1201/9781003422815-4

especially in science class. In addition, programmers use "If" statements as a language to build the game. However, I rarely ever, if ever, heard composers talk about experimentation when making game music. I did hear a lot of "This is how" and "we should do it like". I think sound designers experiment more than composers, which is how the craziest sounds come about. I think the best example to describe this is Ben Burtt's infamous "lightsaber hum sound". He probably thought, "What if I put these hair clippers on the stove and turn the clippers on?" There might have been another "What if" thought that occurred before he arrived there. The point is that the experiment was enacted from the thought.

There are many things I have thought of experimenting with in my compositions.

I Can't Escape: Darkness [2015] – Using Guitar Rig on Vocals. This resulted in some cool, otherworldly dark tones that fit the game very well.

</ reality > [2017] – I tried so many techniques on this. For one, I tried to play guitar again on a couple of pieces from the soundtrack.

"Knowledge of the Ancients", *</reality>* – I connected my Yamaha PSR293 keyboard and played some instrument patches that resulted in blending well with the sound palette texture I created.

"Breaks in Motion", *</reality>* – I decided to sing on the B section of the piece. I was going through a hard break-up and thought that I would sing out my emotions. In addition, I felt that considering the title of the piece and what I was going through, it complemented the music very well.

The tape stop effect represented the breaks in the software that were occurring during the story moment. I had always wanted to incorporate the tape stop effect in a composition, so I was elated to have the opportunity to use it in this piece.

"Discordance", *</reality>* – I applied automation de-tunings for the effect of what was happening in the story. Then, when I hired a Violin player, I had them play the notes in measures 35–36 in tune and I put the MIDI Violins out of tune. This created sonic discordance which tied to the story and song title.

"Epilogue", *</reality>* – I challenged myself to write in one time signature to make it feel like 6/8 but it's only 4/4 to achieve a dynamic music system without middleware.

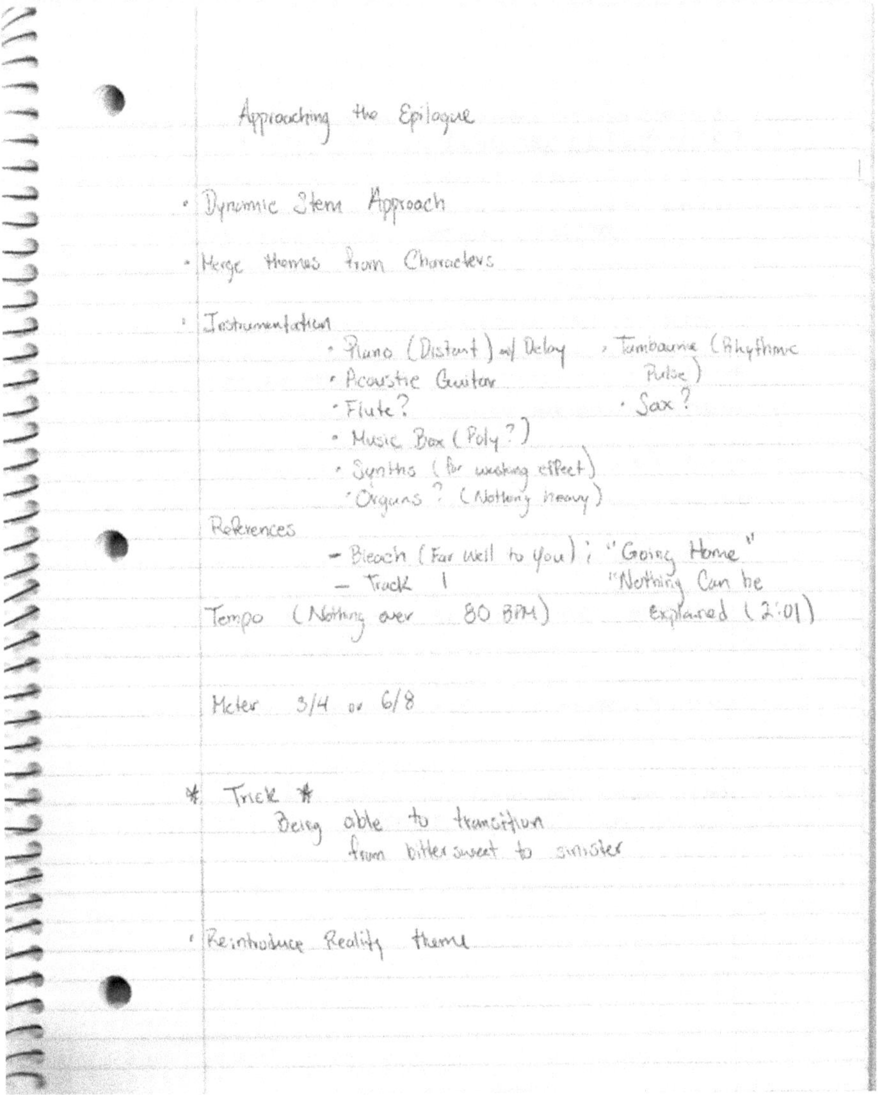

FIGURE 4.1 *</reality>* Journal Entry 12 – Approaching the Epilogue

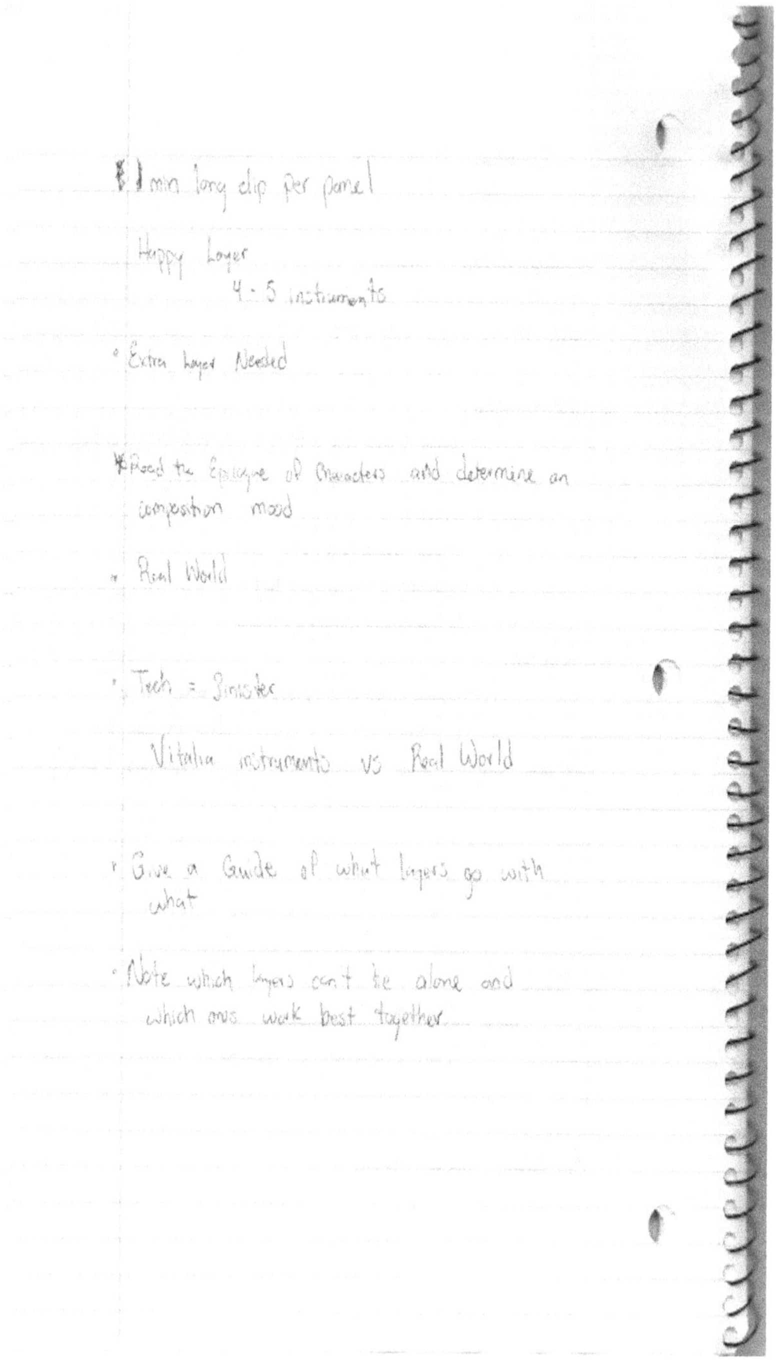

* 1 min long clip per panel

Happy Layer

4-5 instruments

• Extra Layer Needed

* Read the Epilogue of Characters and determine an composition mood

• Real World

• Tech = Sinister

Vitalia instruments vs Real World

• Give a Guide of what layers go with what

• Note which layers can't be alone and which ones work best together

FIGURE 4.2 *</reality>* Journal Entry 12 – Approaching the Epilogue

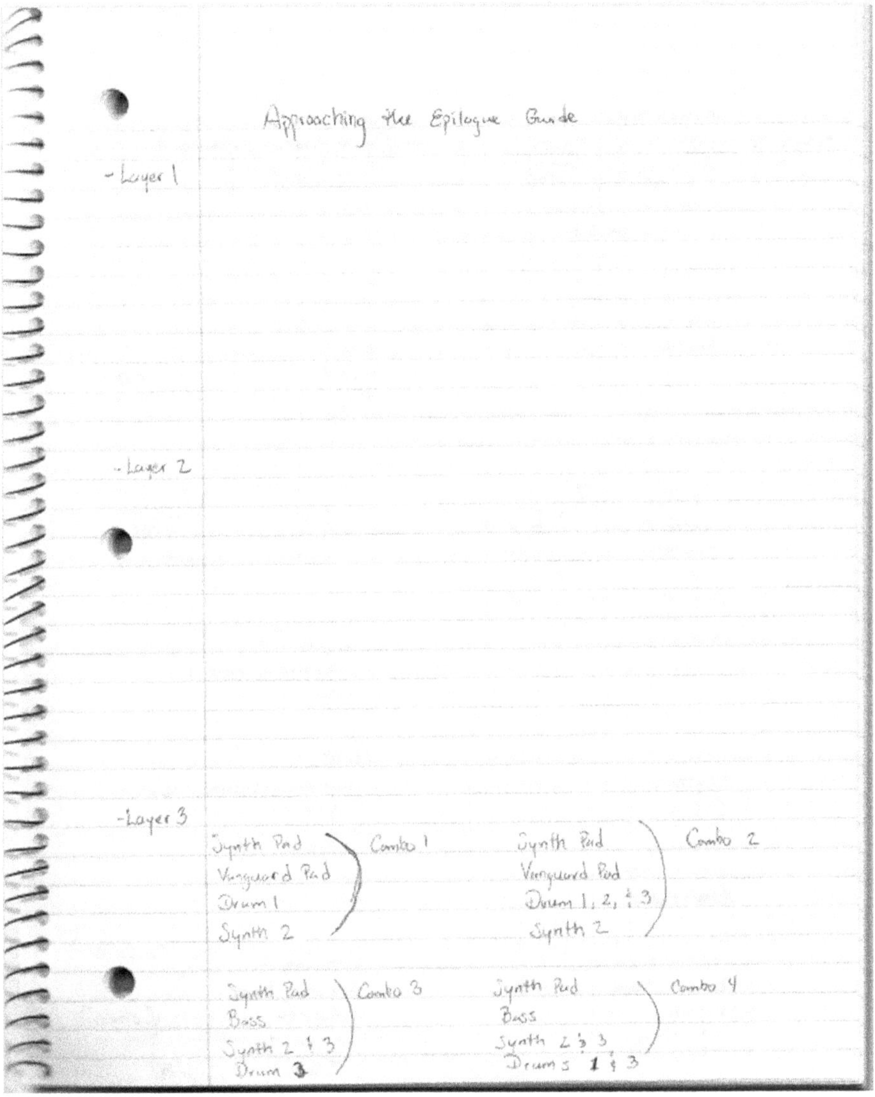

FIGURE 4.3 *</reality>* Journal Entry 12 – Approaching the Epilogue Guide

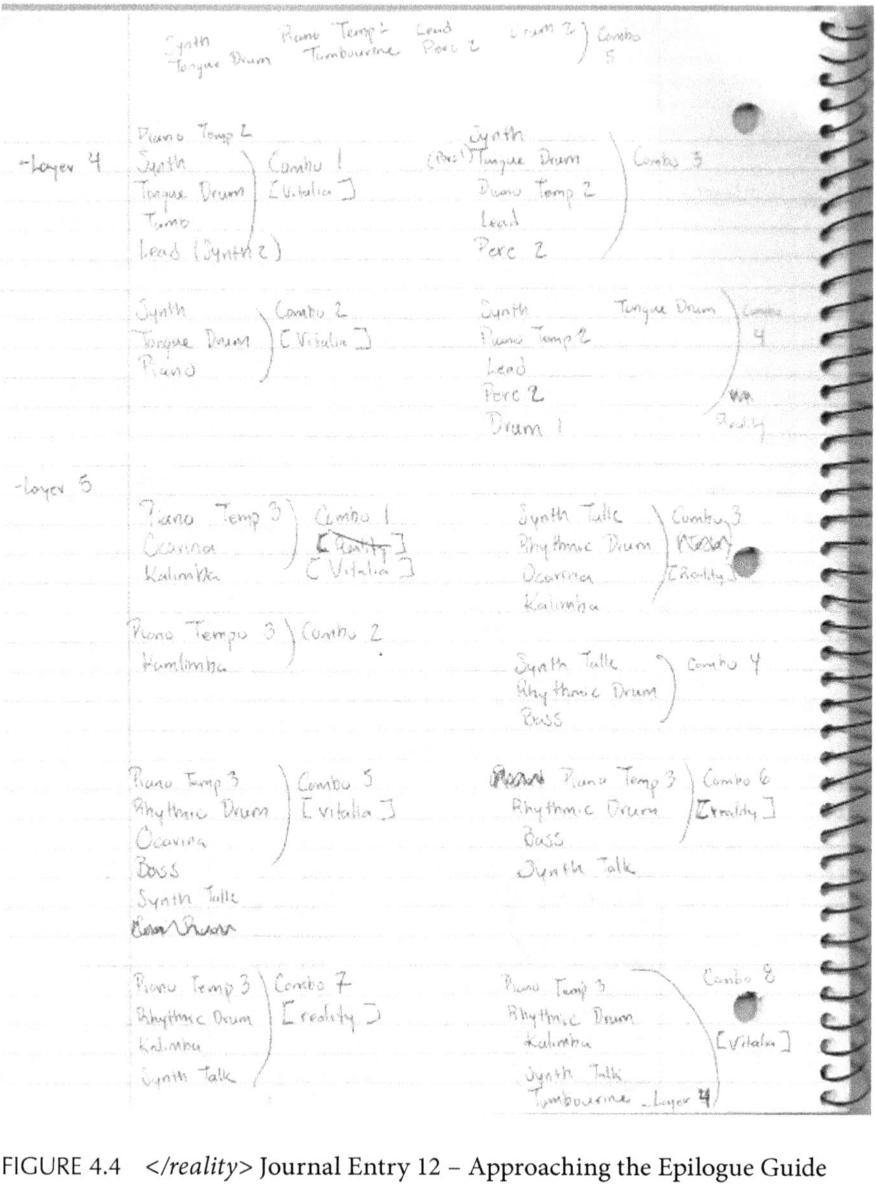

FIGURE 4.4 *</reality>* Journal Entry 12 – Approaching the Epilogue Guide

FIGURE 4.5 </*reality*> Journal Entry 12 – Approaching the Epilogue Guide

Aground [2020] – Coming off the *</reality>* game, I had already started to experiment with odd time signatures, mixed meters and other time signatures that were rarely used in game music. There is still a time signature in the *Aground* soundtrack that only one industry colleague has figured out. No one else has been able to unveil what it is yet.

Number three conflates number one and two along with others and the inspiration you gather. With imagination and experimentation, something incredible happens. You create art of your own that you may not have thought of initially. With this scintilla, you will aplomb and should be able to create more and build upon the spark. This inertia is what designs your signature sound over time. From these points, if you can repeat this process, people will take notice. It may take time, but it will happen.

CHAPTER 5

Class Type(s) – Inaccurate Labels People Give

I noticed a disgusting habit on how some people label each other besides how they introduce themselves and how we wish to be perceived. One year, I was at a Game Developers Conference (GDC) party in a group conversation, and I did an experiment. I was told that I will be remembered by however I introduce myself. So, in the group, I said, "Hi, I'm Chase. I'm a freelance *composer AND sound designer.*" The group acknowledged. Throughout the night, some groups broke off into others but some people whom I met that night already were in those circles. So, in the next group I joined, someone kindly introduced me as a *composer* only not a *sound designer.* Soon after, I went to a different group of people that I did not know. I introduced myself. "Hi, I'm Chase. I'm a *sound designer AND composer.*" The group acknowledged. I left the conversation of that circle and went to another that had someone in it that I had already met. They introduced me as a *sound designer,* not a *composer.* I found this fascinating. Even though I mentioned that I do both roles (at the time), they still only mentioned one of them. One could say that they were trying to get through the round of introductions quickly or simply forgot. This is a fair argument if those are the cases. However, let me continue with another example.

DOI: 10.1201/9781003422815-5

An industry colleague gave an email introduction and said I was a "chip-tune composer" for a project. Now, I specifically got into video game composition and took composition classes to be able to compose in all styles of music genres. I also had other video game music soundtracks released that exhibited genres such as orchestral hybrid, piano, experimental, in addition to *retro-themed* music I had made. I was slightly thrown off by this as I felt that this person did not do their homework. I believe the proper introduction would have said this: "This is Chase! He composes in a lot of music styles including 'chip tune'."

5.1 BEATS THE STEREOTYPE

One time, I was in an interview, where I was under the impression that I was being hired to be a Technical Audio Designer. There was even mention of the opportunity to write music. The interview was going well until one of the interviewers asked about filling in a genre gap of Hip-Hop to help another composer on their staff. They were unable to produce this music style because of the cultural unfamiliarity. This caught me off guard. In my correspondence with them regarding the interview, I never mentioned anything about Hip-Hop before, so they must have heard it in a previous public written or video interview. I was offended, even though I was assured by the other interviewer that they were not trying to offend me. However, I am sure they could probably tell that I was from my facial expressions. I diplomatically explained that although I did have experience with that genre before I started game music, I specifically became a game composer to broaden my music palette, conflate and create multiple musical styles. They were keen enough to politely address the elephant in the room and say that they were not trying to stereotype. It felt awkward and disappointing to be labelled as someone who could make Hip-Hop music when both people saw the work I posted and knew that I did not share any work like that since I have worked in the industry. It left a sour taste in my mouth so much that my energy changed to being uninterested in the remaining time of the interview. However, I sustained my professionalism until the end.

I became a video game composer so that I would have the versatility to indite any style I wanted. So, saying that I make beats is very insulting. I believe, when you decide to be a video game composer, the goal is to be able to write in all kinds of genres for every aspect. Marginalising comes into play when someone says you make "beats" and it is demeaning. Especially, when I have proved to produce other music styles. I have learned and written in different trackers (MOD, Silky, LSDJ, OpenMPT, Fami and ORG Maker) based on some of the limitations of 4 channels and 16 channels. I have composed with rules of four-part harmony, indited 2–3–4-part inventions, fugues, quartets, jazz combos, ensembles and full orchestra. In addition, I have written in the styles of Calypso, Bossa Nova, Ambient, Pop, Trance, House, Rock, Deep House, IDM, Psytrance, D&B, World and so much more.

Notice that Hip-Hop and R&B are not mentioned because I didn't need to learn them by the time I decided to become a video game composer. I already knew it. If I am able to demonstrate that I can write in all those styles successfully and they are published and recognised as their respective style, then I personally find that saying I make "beats" is disrespectful, rude and incorrect. It seems that if you are of a certain skin colour in the industry, some people label you as "beat makers". Before they get to know you, they assume you can only make a certain type of music. For those who don't know, "beats" are classified under the genres of Hip-Hop and R&B.

Why is this? How come it is assumed that I can only produce beats but anyone of a fairly lighter skin colour can compose any other music?

Please stop assuming. If you think it might offend or piss someone off, think very carefully before you speak. If you are insouciant, be prepared for the repercussions and consequences that may follow. Depending on the personality you set off, it could be more than you anticipated.

In another experience, I used to give piano lessons. In doing these lessons, you sometimes get to know the child's parents. In this case, I was talking to the child's mother, who exclaimed she wanted to know more about me. One time, I said to her, "Well, I would have to send you the articles and video blogs to get a deeper understanding. That may help." She replied, "I don't want to know the celebrity, I want to know the piano instructor." I was taken aback and politely responded, "Isn't a celebrity a normal person?" She replied with a "sleeping emoji" and went on to say, "Well, the person I like is the piano instructor soooooo . . ." I was completely silent. In that instant, I had been labelled as who she wanted me to be instead of who I was entirely. None of my accolades, awards, nominations, album releases or any other accomplishments were interesting to her.

In another instance, I was asked for a sound design reel from someone who asked about my music, spent time with me exchanging music in a hallway for an hour and was on a panel with me to discuss . . . can you guess? Music! They even attended a panel I was on that discussed music which was only a month apart from when they were on the panel with me. I have not presented myself as a sound designer to them at all and so I found this to be ultimately disrespectful. Here, I am working with industry colleagues where the discipline is to use their ears, yet they are not listening.

It would seem that people are quick to tell you the class type you are instead of them seeing the class type you are in. So, what does this all mean? Labels suck when they are assumed but only you know who you are. You need to be yourself. Always. You need to find your path and seek your own inspirations until the moment happens where it "clicks" with you instantly. It's that moment of euphoria where you get excited, inspired and emotional all at once. If labels mean something to you, the best thing to do is create your own. Trust me, no one can represent it better than you. This mindset shift spawned in 2011 when I was in community college talking with a classmate.

"Be the first me not the second Beethoven." My friend Nick and I were walking down Moorpark campus college road, and I was exclaiming to him my dream of being the Quincy Jones and Beethoven of game audio. He replied, "Why don't you be the first Chase Bethea?" I never thought of it like that. I suppose when you are in school, we learn about so many heroes, leaders and evangelists and automatically think we want to be like them. We forget that we can be ourselves first and be the first in things as well. Since he told me that in 2011, I never looked back and it started the tenacity, ambition and focus to become the first me in many things in game audio the past decade. The first of anything that is omnipresent in a myriad of categories is in a class of its own. I do aim to be the "Bob" of the Net, the "Mew" of the game and the "Alfred Hitchcock" of video game music. Ultimately, I'm not trying to be the next great comparison, I work consistently at being the "first" me.

CHAPTER 6

"The Next . . ." Is a Trap! Be the First! Be Who You Are!

I recall when I was attending Moorpark College. One mid-afternoon, I said to a friend/colleague on the way to the cafeteria, "I want to be the Beethoven/Quincy Jones of game audio." My friend said to me, "Why don't you just be the first Chase Bethea of game audio?" That thinking right there shifted my entire mindset in that instant. He was right! There was no one like me in the industry. I could and would be the first of many things in the game industry, and so, I set forth on that path to become that. From that day on, I began refining who I was as a human being and started to manifest my destiny.

Make what you want and do not let others decide what or who you "sound" like. When people cannot pinpoint your sound and they start using adjectives, then you truly have found a sound that aligns with your name/brand.

This may or may not take some time. As you share your work with peers and colleagues, they will begin to tell you in an unsolicited manner what it reminds them of and if they truly like it, they will start to compare you to other artists or tell you other artists they like that they believe you should listen to. Look for the pattern.

I read a great quote some years ago that said, "If you compete with others, you will become bitter but if you compete with yourself, you will be better."

DOI: 10.1201/9781003422815-6

CHAPTER 7

"Ism's" Not Advice

7.1 "DO IT BECAUSE YOU LOVE IT"

I think the first time I heard my father say this was in the year 2008. I was in my early to mid-20s. I was at my part-time job with my cousin. He was describing some colleagues who were in the police academy who also did music. One person on the police force was trying this darnedest to become a full-time musician. He envisioned himself doing music full time once he was discovered. However, this did not happen. Alternatively, there were other police officers who still did music in their free time and were still performing. According to my father, they were not concerned with "being discovered", they just wanted to play music and any opportunity that they could they did while keeping the job they had.

"Doing it because you love it" eliminates the stress of it feeling like work and the pressure to make it something sustainable to have a healthy lifestyle.

The reason for him telling me was that he was hearing my passion about starting my career as a composer in games. He told me that I had the right mindset and that should be my focus. He exclaimed that many people get caught up in the "fame illusion". This means that they want to do something because they believe it will make them famous and that this is what trips people up. "Do it because you love it and if something else comes of it then that's icing on the cake," he said.

To this day, I believe in this mantra as it has been practiced in my everyday routine. When I get booked for interviews and I discuss my work, you hear the passion in my voice. I love this industry a lot. I do it because I love

DOI: 10.1201/9781003422815-7

it. Sometimes love hurts a lot too because it does not always reciprocate. However, I fully understand this comes with the territory. I suppose my love may be unconditional in this form. I have already given so much. Fame is not a focus but doing great work for generations to be impacted and enjoyed is.

If you get offered anything else, then it is a bonus. You do not need anyone to tell you how good an engineer or composer you are. Your skills, talent and art speak for itself. It boils down to confidence. Confidence does not equal arrogance. You can be confident and humble.

"The quality of patience with yourself is the key to seeing your options vividly."

I wrote this many years ago on my Facebook page. Although I cannot recall the reason I wrote this, as I reflect on it now, I find it to be sound advice.

How I apply this "ism" now is in this age/era, everything is "go, go, go". There are shorter attention spans, social media bombardment, sales pitches and deals on items left and right. The popular proverbial phrase is that "Patience is a virtue" and the definition of a virtue is *a behaviour showing high moral standard.* In a busy world, we must condition ourselves to slow down. I believe that a high moral standard of patience is lost in most of humanity. We are currently conditioned to have instant gratification. However, if we practiced patience, the world around us would slow down. Our minds begin to open up and wander. Once you build upon this

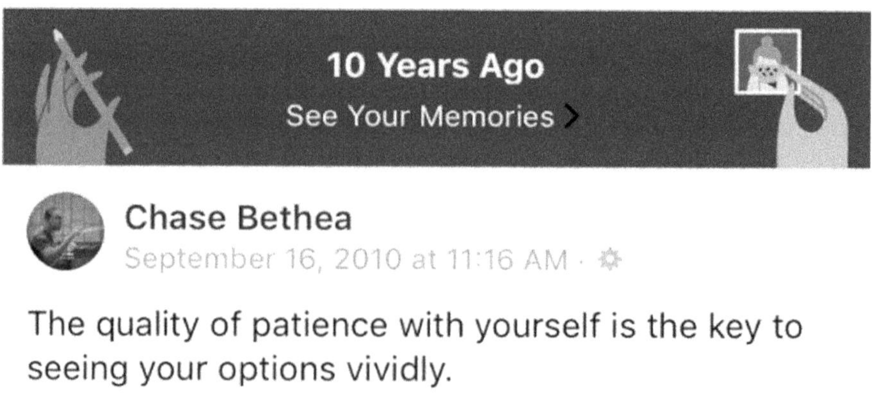

FIGURE 7.1 The Quality of Patience

practice, the quality enhances. You will find that decision, something our brains do every second of every day while we are conscious, becomes more fluid. Problem-solving is more simplified and less stressful. Day-to-day tasks are accomplished with finesse and ease. Creative ideas would spark more naturally and fluidly. I would feel less inundated. Clouded judgement will not occur as much if at all. Whenever I was impatient, internal chaos was bound to ensue, and I was constantly in a maelstrom.

Over time, I learned to evaluate and balance professionalism better. When emails would come in, I would ask myself, "How important are they to be responded to?" When I attended CSUN (California State University, Northridge), the Head of Media Composition told us, "Professional emails should be responded to within 24 hours." While some people appreciated these prompt replies, others did not reciprocate, and this caused stress. There was a possibility that the email professionalism was not on par. So, I learned that those people were either busy or practicing what I learned to do which was slowing down and building quality. Some emails do need prompt replies, but the craft comes into discerning which ones those are. In addition, I became patient when receiving those emails and would be pleasantly surprised if after weeks or months, I would see a reply.

We all have a certain amount of patience. Due to people's decisions that impact our lives, we lose that over time. I found that rebuilding patience is the key to developing quality in the behaviour. Many people do not believe this, but *Dark Souls* is where I rebuild that patience. Since the game is so punishable with its gameplay, I can see the core design is to tell people to slow down and take their time. This is not a "hack n' slash". As I mentioned before in another chapter, the boss fights and/or most of these battle encounters are where the patience meter is built. If you get frustrated with the game, it's a common user error. The game went gold and shipped many years ago, with millions of copies sold. Many people beat it several times over. Now it is your turn. So, if you rage quit, you lost patience with yourself, the game did not. Once I overcame that boss fight and/or beat the game, I had this grandiose feeling of accomplishment I got from the victory. There was something else happening, a lesson. I taught myself how to dodge, weave, look for patterns, stay calm, persevere and endure. When an attack style did not work, I pivoted, did some level grinding and returned to the fight until the challenge was conquered. No one else did that for me. The controller was in my hands. This is how I rebuilt, and once I completed that process, the quality was refined. Through this process, I saw my options to defeat the enemies and boss in a clear form, and I enacted them. I applied these lessons and tactics to people who had delayed responses or did not reply at all, opportunities that appeared to ramp up quickly and then halted as well as project cycles that were not the most efficient.

Those triumphant moments are summarised in that year-long reply for being denied an assistant position to becoming a good friend with an AAA composer that I can shoot the breeze with and get hired to subcontract on one of their projects. Another year-long correspondence comes from this being the first video game music article published in a nationwide magazine in 20 years. Wanting to be a guest on a game audio podcast to being a panellist and then eventually being a guest years later. When I was turned down from audio company collaborations to now being sponsored by some of the top audio gear and software companies in the world. Good things come to those who wait, and greater things come to those who have waited longer.

7.2 "YOU ARE NEVER LATE FOR ART; ART IS ON TIME FOR YOU"

This quote was conceived due to a disrespectful experience. An industry colleague shamed me, and a game was partially spoiled for not playing a game in a time period he felt I should have played. "The game has been out for 15 years. You should have played it by now," he said. I am sorry. I did not know I was on your time schedule of living life and playing games, asshole! Imagine telling your child or any child, any entertainment media (movies, games, music, etc.) that has been out before they were born, that they should have played, seen or heard it by now. The inconsideration is wild! In addition, I have seen others feel guilty by preface by saying, "I know I'm late to play, see or listen to this" or they apologise.

Why should they have to do that? You should not have to apologise for living your life at *your* pace. Maybe you had a family member go through cancer and that took up your time and energy. Maybe the hype was overrated for that entertainment when it was released, and you were not into it. Maybe you genuinely missed it because you were busy with something else. Maybe you could not afford it. In the 90s, games used to cost $70. Some consoles, computers and gaming handhelds were $799.99. Not every family was affluent enough to purchase one for their household along with games and not every child was fortunate to even have friends or privileges due to parental restrictions where they could go to a house where those games were accessible. So, let's knock it off with spoiling art and guilt-tripping people because *you* think "they had time" to consume it. Take some acknowledgement and cognizance that other life events occur outside yours.

7.3 "THE SKILL WAS HONED BUT THE TALENT WAS BORN"

I believe that everyone is born with some form of talent, but some talent may need to be refined as it may have some rough edges. Not everyone is born a Mozart. So, through talent, you can build skills, and once they are combined, it can be great.

Skills that you learn are practiced, repeated and you must put in the time and effort to get good at what you put your mind to. However, when you are born with the gift and have the talent, some people do not need to put a lot of time and/or effort into it. They can just do it. They can get on stage and rock a performance or a presentation. They can pick up and learn an instrument because they have perfect pitch. Some are born with many talents but may not be good at many skills. There comes a time when the quote by Tim Notke comes in, "Hard work beats talent when talent doesn't work hard." However, there will come a time, if the skills are refined, they will combine and the talent within will shine.

CHAPTER 8

Certain Tips Often Spoken but Didn't Stand True

"If a previous colleague remembers your 'awesome sounds' on a project and that you are thoroughly nice person to have on the team, they might recommend you in the future."

"If you build a good relationship with your clients, they'll come back to you for their next project." – (A sound effect article – 10 Tips for Freelancers)

I added previous clients to newsletters so that they could keep up with my work. I also reached out to previous clients, people I did game jams with and more. In my ten years, I always had to start over from scratch by meeting someone new in order to procure work. I was under the facade that once I worked with a client, they would rehire me, and only two out of the many did. So, the statement, "building a good relationship and the client will come back to you" does hold true in some way but the mistake I made was thinking every person that I worked with would do the same.

My first gig, the developer retired from game development. Another gig, the developer required more work from me but did not want to pay me. Another developer decided to seek full-time work at a game studio, another client, as best I built the relationship with the team and the CEO (so I thought), and the majority quit and went to other studios including

DOI: 10.1201/9781003422815-8

the producer, and the CEO never replied to my email. Now, maybe my practices of going about it could have been wrong. All I would do is reach out to see if they were working on anything new and to keep me in mind. It was not for lack of trying and following up but unfortunately, I have to assume that if I never get the response after a few follow-up emails, then the message that they are sending is that they are not interested in continuing a collaboration.

So, what does a person do? Quit? In my case, I sure have thought about it several times. However, what I did decide was to get better at business. At first, I wanted to study human psychology to determine why people think the way they do. I thought that by learning this, I could get closer to the mindset that people have who run these businesses. However, I quickly decided that it would be too time-consuming, daunting, and possibly uninspirational to continue working in the game industry once I discovered the truth about those mindsets. Instead, I focused my efforts on the things I already knew about business from my ten years working in retail and furthering my knowledge by reading about business. In turn, this happened to unveil some psychology about the business mindset while sharing healthy business practices. This proved to be quite useful as I was now covering all the bases.

CHAPTER 9

Math versus Mentality

This chapter is going to make sense to some people but probably not to most. If you have gotten this far in the book, you have probably noticed that I have been talking a lot about mentality. Ironically, we work with some of the most brilliant people in the industry, most of whom can do math and basic math at that. However, it does not seem that once the math is calculated, that the mentality changes.

A game studio reached out to me, wanting me to score their game. The two of creative directors have a "day job" where they work at one of the top media companies in the states. I was told that everyone on the team works a "day job". It is their first game studio that they started, and they had no prior experience working with a composer before.

They had a successful crowdfunding campaign. When I did the research about the campaign, I allocated the amount that usually should be budgeted for the soundtrack. The campaign did not outline the budget for the soundtrack until six tiers above it being funded and they made over half a million dollars in crowdfunding.

They requested a quote for 30–40 tracks and the length of each track to be one minute each. I sent them a quote, and then they asked for a discounted quote, and it was given to them.

A week or so later, I was briefed that they were hiring another composer. I thought to myself, okay, that cuts into the audio budget but since they made over half a million dollars, the math still works out.

Then, they approached me wanting to do an exclusive buyout deal. This gave me some reservations. I explained to them that in order to do that

DOI: 10.1201/9781003422815-9

deal, it would be 3xs the rate amount. Their response was that they could not afford that and offered a different number and a bonus.

I proceeded to do the math. If they bought out the music, I would not be able to do the following:

1. Re-license the music.
2. Do performances with the music.
3. Earn royalties on soundtrack sales.

I am the one, as the artist/composer, who loses here. I do not see the half a million dollars plus in sales, they do.

I figured if I did the math, the numbers would give me the answer. I would need a certain percentage I deem to be fair to make up for the loss of what they could not afford the buyout to be.

The buyout was close to 40k. I thought, if I ask these questions, and they come back with the right numbers or close, it would determine how I would move forward. These were my questions.

Question 1. Will there still be a definite 30 tracks needed? If not, what's the minimum/maximum approximate range amount?

Their answer: Now their approach was assigning tracks via batches with separate contracts. They explained that each batch would have 10–11 tracks, for a total *potential* of 21 tracks. (Remember, they initially asked for a quote for up to 40 tracks. It is very interesting how the number keeps creeping down.) The initial contract would encompass one batch to start, containing 10 tracks.

In my opinion, this feels like they are feeling me out and I am still in the demo process. I sensed that if they did not like what I did within the 10 pieces I indite, they could replace me and hopefully with someone and something better. In addition, salvage the remaining tracks to match their creative vision.

Question 2. There was a mention of paying a bonus. I asked if they could clarify if that bonus is from game sales? Soundtrack sales or both? (game sales and soundtrack sales). Also, will that be gross sales? When will this be paid? Monthly? Quarterly?

Question 3. I asked if they could clarify the number after which that bonus will come in? i.e. (After 5k in game sales soundtrack sales or both then bonus of x amount will be sent)

Question 4. I asked to clarify which sales type it is (game sales, soundtrack sales or both). What was the percentage? 5%, 10%, 15%, 20%?

Question 5. I asked what the percentage of soundtrack sales split would be. 60/40, 70/30, 50/50?

Not only did they copy, paste and colour code my questions but they tried to lump the questions together, figuring they were answering them.

Their answer:

Questions 2, 3, 4, 5

The bonus will be a one-time flat-fee bonus of $150 per minute of music once 3000 copies of the original soundtrack are sold.

I was confused how we went from a potential 21 tracks at specific per finished minute to a shipped game and a new rate of $150.00 per finished minute.

I asked if there was more music to write after the game shipped. The copies sold did not make sense to me unless there was DLC or more chapters to write music for after the game shipped. I requested a breakdown and they replied.

> If there are 21 minutes of music made for the OST (original soundtrack), then once the OST has 3,000 units sold, a bonus of $150/minute would be distributed to the composer for the 21 minutes of completed work. This is in addition to the agreed per finished minute rate paid up front.

Wow! Are you on the jog with me yet? The game crowdfunded over half a million. Their crowdfunding asking goal was close to 100k with no original soundtrack in mind listed within that goal. It was only to fund the game. It is a general rule of thumb to allocate 10% of the budget to audio. That number in relation to this game's budget is between 70k and 80k which they reached and beyond. Their full tier requests were close to

400k, and they superseded that almost two times over. Not only that, did you notice how they did not answer my other questions? Also, they get to determine the price of the soundtrack on all platforms. That price could be anywhere from \$7.00–\$30.00 per platform. Why 3,000? That number seemed quite high to me.

Question 6. I asked, if they could please verify the comfortable cap number or the years to stop receiving royalties? i.e. a year cap of eight years.

Question 7. I asked if there was not a year cap that can be estimated, was there a number cap? Alternatively, if there was an option to determine the year cap or the number, whichever comes first?

Their answer:

Questions 6, 7

Unfortunately, we do not have the bandwidth to offer royalties for any duration at this time.

From there, I exclaimed my concern with the terms and ambiguity. They replied that they understand and *while they would've loved to find a middle ground, my interest and comfort have always been a top priority.*

Bullshit! They did not answer all my questions. So, there was no "middle ground". I offered so many options to reach a consensus and there was no interest in them, or those questions would have been answered.

All of these problems surfaced when they decided that they wanted exclusive rights to the music. It was a brand-new small studio team trying to operate at an AAA level with fear. Bad news bears.

My worth is based on my 7,485 days of experience, multiple awards won for my soundtracks for games, multiple published articles in nationwide and global magazines as well as books and my decade experience in guest speaking at some of the top game conferences including being a keynote speaker.

Studios of all sizes *need* to do proper market research to determine what the proper rate per game discipline is, especially in game audio. This ignorance is not bliss or acceptable.

I sensed there was a lot of fear with the people at this studio. They could have had a lawyer to avoid the fear but maybe they did not want to pay for a lawyer either.

Here are some things that could have been in the contract to cover themselves.

- Composer will not be allowed to form another studio and use the music of this IP (Intellectual Property).
- Year caps (Composer only gets paid up to x amount of years).
- Number cap (Composer will only receive royalties up to x amount).
- Percentages (Composer will only receive this percentage from this specific type of sales, etc.).

So, the math could have worked out, but I see it comes down to mentality. The mentality to pay for a lawyer, hire part-time help with administrative tasks, lock in a percentage to share that would be fair for both parties, and weigh the pros and cons of the value I brought to the table to elevate the game even further. I offered to do dynamic music design which they were excited for as no one on the team thought of it and split live performances of the soundtrack sales.

It is quite apparent that some people want to get what they want instead of the long term of the deal.

So, they could potentially have bought the exclusive rights if they

1. Drop the other composer. Side note: (They explained to me that the composer was new to games and never wrote for the medium before). The studio also made the assumption that I could not handle the full soundtrack on my own (getting an understanding of how fast I could write, meeting milestones/deadlines, etc.). They never asked me, giving me the opportunity to say yes or no.
2. Allocated more money to the music budget.

I have a saying called "Toledo Bull". It is to describe when something is a massive red flag. When a matador is in the bull pen, they sometimes have a red cape. It appears to be as large as a flag, regardless of when that bull sees it and charges, the matador's life is on the line. I normally grade concerns with football penalty terms. For example, yellow card, orange card and red card. Depending on the concerns and the situation escalated past the cards, then I call it a red flag and finally a "Toledo Bull".

This situation started as a yellow card once I was told another composer was part of a team. I will be discussing my experience about that in a later chapter. Then, it moved to an orange card when I was told they wanted to buy the exclusive rights. It became a red card when they mentioned 3,000 units sold with a low per finished minute rate bonus. It was a red flag when they circumvented most of my questions, had excuses for what I gathered to be a cop out and a full "Toldedo Bull" when I assessed the half-a-million-dollar crowdfund campaign and the "day jobs" that they had at a specific company.

As I have grown and traversed this industry, I have worked out many deals for writing music for games. Many with small teams. We have worked things out. I have only had my music "exclusive" to one game and even we worked out a soundtrack deal (Thank you, Molten Tomato). I have yet to work with a team that had a successful crowdfunding campaign with solid "day jobs", started a studio and approached me with the numbers and terms this studio did. I would have expected this from the small team that did not have a successful crowdfunding campaign and was paying out of their pocket to fund the entire game.

The mentality is paramount. However, the math has to make sense. Numbers do not lie and normally the numbers will force someone to change their mentality.

CHAPTER 10

Corrupted Save Files – The Dead Ends of What I Thought Was Going to Be a Good Connection

In 2022, I found myself scrolling through my phone on Mother's Day to wish my friends who were mothers, Happy Mother's Day. What I discovered was besides the fact that I didn't know as many mothers directly anymore, there was also a bunch of other names that were in my phone that I never talked to. A lot of them were industry connections that I thought would lead to future work. Not for a lack of trying or hustling but simply people not reaching back out to me when I reached out to them multiple times. It wasn't like they had passed away (thankfully), as I would do my due diligence in researching them on social media to see how they were doing, but it seemed as though they didn't care to even respond. Life gets busy but if the follow-ups go from every two weeks to bimonthly and after reaching out a few times nothing is reciprocated. I think it becomes clear that the connection you thought was going somewhere isn't going anywhere. It sucks too.

I recall setting up a booth at my first The MIX at E3 2019 event as a developer, stepping in for the other team members who could not be there.

DOI: 10.1201/9781003422815-10

FIGURE 10.1 E3 2019 The MIX Booth Set-up

Next to me was another developer, after some hours passed, I decided to talk to him as I had noticed that he and Metal Jesus had a solid 20-minute conversation. I got to know the developer a little more, found out he was from Texas and that Metal Jesus was following his game due to the Metroidvania style. As the night progressed, we joked and laughed. It was a good time. The following day, I saw him eating breakfast at the convention centre cafe area. I asked if I could sit with him and he obliged. We talked some more and connected on a couple of other topics. He agreed to keep in touch and with me being who I am, I knew I could do that. I followed up with a couple of emails a few weeks after E3. I didn't hear anything back. I recall sending a couple of more emails and even a couple of texts some months afterwards. Meanwhile, checking his social media to see if everything was good with them and it was. They were still very active on social media. I still received emails that his game was on sale. I saw he was posting about it. So, I thought, "What the hell?" Why pretend to be nice and say you'll do something if you have zero interest in it from the gate? It didn't make sense. The guy was so cool (or so I thought). I guess he was just "frontin". One of those people who probably thinks with this mentality, "I don't want to hurt this person's feelings, so I'll be nice right now". The truth is that shit is nocuous and stings/hurts more in the long run. No one likes being led on.

There was a developer I was introduced to during an indie game movie premiere, "Game Loading – Rise of the Indies". He was working on a very cool accessibility game and was interested in collaborating on his next accessibility game. Before collaborating, he and I hung out a few times as he invited me over to his house. We connected on both being from the Midwest, playing the "Legend of Zelda Master Quest" as he shared with me the history of its release. The real gaming connection occurred when we played NBA Jam Sega Genesis. We were both very competitive and tied in our matches. This made the collaboration on his project smoother. We were able to communicate and create with ease. Unfortunately, after we finished the project demo to submit to an indie game festival, he had to move back to his home state to sustain. He and I said we would keep in touch, and we would continue to polish the game and ship it. When I said I did my part, I did it. I texted, I called, I emailed within reason every two weeks to a month or two months. To my surprise, I never heard from them. He completely disappeared for about eight years. No replies anywhere. I thought the worst might have happened until one day in June 2023. Out of nowhere, my posts were being liked on social media. What are his reasons for doing what he did? Who knows. What I do know is that actions sucked and affected me in a negative way. The industry has enough psychological issues to address but if people cannot keep it honest and say things like, "I'm sorry I will not be able to work on the game anymore," or "Our collaboration will no longer be able to work out but I'm happy to stay friends." Whatever the reasoning is, saying nothing and ignoring isn't always the solution, especially if the last words that were exchanged were on good terms.

When I entered this field, I used to think that if I helped people, they would return the favour. That was not the case. Most people found themselves "too busy" to help and they did not tell me to my face. They just did not respond. Even when I followed up. There was no response. It forced me to stop asking for help. So, whenever I hear about "collaborations" and working with others, I'm very hesitant. As I found out very early in my career that most people are not reliable and do not have the same ethics as I do.

Imagine you put all your time into a game, levelling up, sidequesting, grinding to craft ultima weapons, and then your save gets corrupted. It feels the same, you put the time in to build a relationship, talk, joke and laugh, find a similar connection to make a friend and the "save point" of where you were in that connection is corrupted due to their unkind and possibly ignorant actions to not reciprocate in continuing the friendship journey. I cannot count how many times in the decade this has happened to me. And if you are an avid game player like me, if your save gets corrupted, you find yourself not wanting to play that game anymore. It leaves me jaded from the "networking/making friends" experience. It's only so much energy (HP) that I have in the world and doing the same thing over and over with new people only to have another corrupted save file is arduous and becomes depressing. It comes to the point now that when I go through my contacts and I see that name, I cannot remember it. In addition, if I did not take good notes or they don't have a social media account with their name or handle, then that corrupted save point has to be deleted. It didn't have to be that way. It could have been a good multiplayer experience, meaning they reciprocate the communication within the initial connection to building a friendship. Even if we never worked together. Unfortunately, I have heard a lot of "corrupted save" stories from others instead of a change in game taste, meaning the friendship grew apart due to life circumstances or other situations. I can accept the change in game taste because at least most of the time there was a friendship link to begin with. What I will not ever respect is putting the time into someone only to be ignored later on. People in the industry need to learn the language of soft rejection. It saves everyone's time. You're not responsible for their mental state. You are responsible for your own. So, if you're approached to connect and you don't feel it, then kindly decline. Don't be an asshole. Learn the language that lets them down easy. The majority of the time, they will respect you in the long run. Their save states matter just as much as yours. Their mental state will be happier long term too. Our industry is hard enough to solve technical problems, making choices like these on a personal level makes it a little easier to manage and burn others out when they don't deserve it.

CHAPTER 11

Continue?

At many points in my career, I felt lost. I felt like quitting game audio. I discovered that it wasn't as sustainable as I hoped unless a game took off, the composer became popular, and AAA studios continuously contracted you. I knew that if I said I was officially quitting, people may say, "Don't quit, keep trying." I put the blame on myself because I chose this path which was partially why I was feeling depressed, but I did not know what else to do. I endlessly kept pushing myself to learn more nonetheless I still felt lost. I did not know what I was doing right or wrong. However, I knew something was not working and I had to figure it out soon.

In 2016, after working on the "</reality>" soundtrack, I wanted to quit the field. I was going through a really terrible break-up with a girl. Even though the break-up was not the complete impetus for me not wanting to continue on in the video game industry, the feeling of loss made me feel like I was going to lose it all. The best way to describe it would be to hit your head on a hard surface and lose your memory. The fear of loss is intense. I recall waking up multiple mornings and my heart felt like it was skipping beats. There were heart murmurs and many anxiety attacks that enacted my vertigo. So, I started to believe that I was not cut out for this industry anymore. I felt that I did not have any more music in me. I did not know what was going on. I put years of effort into the romantic relationship and similarly I put more years of exertion into my craft/career. I was so distracted from the moment of the situation. I went from living in a nice condo to living in a garage. I believe the wake-up call for me was that I could lose the rest of what I had built in my career if I did not find

DOI: 10.1201/9781003422815-11

work and finish uni. Nonetheless, through the pain and heartache, I truly discovered that I am a warrior, a survivor and a lot stronger than I thought I was. It is weird being on the other side of it now that I chose to continue on the unpaved path. The confidence is completely solidified to know that I have the strength to overcome more adversity. However, it is a whole different feeling when you are really in it. Because when you ask yourself to retry, the passion within is sometimes not enough to press on. For many, this would have been the "rage quit" or the "I tap out" point. These are the times I wished I had a Game Genie or GameShark to give me an extra heart or extra lives.

When I shipped "</reality>", I recall sitting outside in the backyard in a lawn chair at 6:30 pm. I poured a glass of wine, looked in the sky, thanked God and the universe, took a couple of sips and let some tears run down my face. I was thankful that I made it through. It was the closest I ever cut it. There were lots of breakdowns that occurred when inditing the music. My drive was to deliver and not to let my professionalism falter. I knew the developers and Kickstarter backers were counting on me and I was not going to let them down.

In giving inspiration, one needs to receive inspiration. If one runs out of inspiration because they gave it their all, what is left to do? What do they have to re-up with? I know the encouragement is to "Keep on Pushing! Keep on grinding. Keep going." At some point, though, some major results have to come into play. Just as we do in games, it's okay to just press "pause". We press play every time we go to work and some of us do bonus levels (side gigs and volunteer work) on top of the daily grind. We have to learn to press pause and press it more often so that we can decide to continue.

One part of the solution was having the right members in your party. My mum would send me encouraging messages. My father bluntly told me that if I quit school and the industry, all the work I did would be for nothing. My grandmother and my brother Efosa were a solid soundboard and passed no judgement. The few peers I trusted in uni aided in the positive distraction to endure the day-to-day struggle.

The other part of the solution I found to persevere was to look back at the save states. I cogitated on how far I had come in my career (several games shipped, soundtracks released, mentions on Destructoid, nominated among top game composers in the industry and made the Dean's list each semester since enrollment). These were my "save states" and I did it all while attending uni and trying to have a romantic relationship. I had chosen ultra-hard mode. Although I failed at the relationship, and almost quit school too, I chose to learn from it. My lesson was to be happy with what I currently had, and I had life. My mental focus was that if I could survive today, I can survive tomorrow. Survival mode turned into thriving mode. The "</reality>" soundtrack had to get done because Kickstarter backers paid for it. It was imperative that I graduated, which meant my senior recital had to be planned, produced and executed. I discerned that I had already put too many grind time hours in the other areas of my life, and I would complete the challenge mode I started on. I believed in not only continuing but finishing strong and with a great ending.

CHAPTER 12

Failed Level Skips – How My Career Could Have Advanced Sooner

A lot of people dropped the ball on me. I always came through on my part but there have been false promises and a lack of honesty that have come from others. These parties did not take responsibility/accountability to be upfront to say they could not uphold their part of the bargain with what they said they would do. The alternative perspective argument that some will think of will be "they owe me nothing", however, some of these people came to me first about these opportunities and offers. If they followed through with it, I believe it could have levelled up my career tremendously. Here are some stories that correlate to that. I call them "Failed level skips".

12.1 CODENAME SILVERBACK WEREWOLF STUDIOS

In 2013, I applied for a composer position. It was a revenue share project, and during this time in games, revenue share seemed to be very promising. The project lead of the studio apparently liked my work and wanted to bring me on board along with another composer. They were making a game that was in the style of *Metal Gear Solid*. In fact, they were trying to copy *Metal Gear Solid* completely. Since I thought that the *Metal Gear Solid* franchise was popular, I had believed that this would be a game if I

DOI: 10.1201/9781003422815-12

did a solid orchestral score, that would take my career to the next level. The project had very talented voice actors, level design and concept artists.

It wasn't too long after I was on the project that I learned that this game has been in development for ten years. A small group of people started the concept in high school, and once they had graduated, they continued to work on the game. This was an immediate "Toledo bull". Although their efforts in trying to create a studio and make something happen, the lack of maturity and social etiquette showed in terms of competency and management.

After a year on the project, I had learned that they were not really a fan of my music as they constantly were always implementing the other composer's work and giving them praise. However, at the same time, they continued to ask me to write music for "just in case purposes". Meaning, if they could use it in the game, they wanted the opportunity and the liberty to do so. However, I still did not receive any accolades for my work ethic of at least delivering. It turned out that they really wanted me to be an Audio Director. My roles increased from writing some in-game music to doing sound design, editing, voice-over work and making audio logs for the game. The first composer who started with me left the project and another composer was brought on board. I had to oversee his work, and the project leads chose his work over mine. The leads realised how long it was taking to make the game and pivoted to release a smaller version of the game. This was actually the tutorial from the main game, but they masked it. The gameplay mimicked *Metal Gear Solid* Special Missions (PS1). Even in this clone release, none of my music had been implemented. My hope and goal were to use the music that made it into the game in a demo reel and leverage it to get a paying gig, but that opportunity never came.

Around the third year of being on the project, things came to a head. One of the project leads was scheduling and not honouring meeting times by not showing up and with no remorse or follow-up. At this point, I determined with all the work that I had been consistently delivering on time for years that it was ultimately disrespectful. I happily resigned from the project.

I believe all the project leads should have done was be transpicuous if there was a bias about how they felt about my work. All they had to say was that they thought my music was good, but they did not think it was good enough to be used in the game. Even though it may be harsh, it is easier to accept the truth rather than some underhanded sneakiness, lead ons and lies. If something is creatively not working, we should make the effort to be open and ready to have that conversation, rather than it being a surprise to that person. If the role was reversed, and if it was done to them, I am almost certain they would not like it. However, as I mentioned before, the lack of maturity greatly showed. I witnessed many talented and skilled voice actors, artists and other people in game design disciplines leave the project.

12.2 DOG EAT DOG STUDIOS

I went to GDC in 2017 or 2018. I recall attending an event called CGX (Canadian Games Expo). I met a developer by the name of "K". This studio's code name is "Dog Eat Dog Studios". The developer and I talked about music for their upcoming project. I was a little excited, but I tempered my enthusiasm just because of previous experiences that I had with developers. After GDC, I followed up with an email and a small demo to showcase my vision for the project after what they had briefly described to me at our in-person discussion. "K" liked the demo and offered me a contract based on the rate that I told them.

May 22, 2018, 4:43 PM

to me

Is a start date of Monday, June 4th good for you? I know you had some stuff to finish up before we really get going?

Get Outlook for iOS

...

FIGURE 12.1 K Email Correspondence

We both signed the contract. At this point, it felt like it was too good to be true. This is my first GDC contract that I acquired. It only took several years. Nonetheless, I was elated. "K" was very excited to bring me onto the team and exclaimed that they would fly me out to Canada to visit the studio and the rest of the team periodically during the development process. This appeared to be a proper gig, and I was very enthused to be part of it. We agreed upon a start date, and I was proactive in asking if I would have an outline of duties per week.

Chase Bethea <chasebethea@gmail.com> May 22, 2018, 4:53 PM

Yea, June 4th works. Will I have an outline of duties per week?

...

FIGURE 12.2 K Email Correspondence

Well, the first month will be pretty experimental as we find the right groove and get some promotional bits together

Tbh, it may be a month or two before we are far enough along to have a solid grasp of the audio scope, and can generate final game assets

But we can certainly figure out the best way forward together

K

Get Outlook for iOS

FIGURE 12.3 K Email Correspondence

He replied, "The first month will be pretty experimental as we refined the great groove and got some promotional bits together" (Figure 12.3). Unfortunately, from there the problems began.

I started on the main theme. "K" took a week to get back to me.

Chase Bethea

Okay that makes sense. That will work quite well

As we discussed before that is okay too. I figured since the promo work was getting under way

I'm happy to figure it out with you

FIGURE 12.4 K Email Correspondence

Main Theme

Chase Bethea

Hey

Here is a mock-up of the main theme that I started. It's not finished yet A work in progress) but I wanted to give you an idea

Kindly,
Chase Bethea
Composer/Sound Designer
Twitter: @chasebethea

One attachment · Scanned by Gmail

FIGURE 12.5 K Email Correspondence

I sent a revised version based on their feedback.

Hey Chase,

Sorry for dropping off the planet - we just finished our big design week, and it was pretty intense but super productive!

I like the overall flavour of this theme, but it's a bit too regularly discordant. I'd like it to be more melodic/euphoric. I don't mind a touch of discord in the middle to suggest the mental health struggles, but it should be much more up beat overall

I also like the tempo you introduce to suggest action, but I feel it's too driven by the electronic percussion - I'd like to see more of this driven by a baseline instead, so it's more musical

I apologize for my non musical language terms - let me know if you're free this week anytime and we can have a chat about it so we're on the same page and then we can make adjustments!

Talk soon

FIGURE 12.6 K Email Correspondence

"K" took another week to reply. He exclaimed that there was "a little funding hiccup."

Chase Bethea

Hey

Here is the revised version. I listened to your references for the basslines that you sent and I also listened a bunch to Knights of Sidonia. I found in Knights of Sidonia the undertone driving bass so I added that but kept it tucked underneath so that it's not so club-like. In addition, I heard in the Conan reference that the horns were giving that euphoric feel and adding more excitement/energy so I added those.

Let me know your thoughts. I hope the con went well and you are well rested. Talk to you soon.

Kind Wishes,
Chase Bethea
Composer/Sound Designer
www.chasebethea.com
Twitter: @chasebethea

One attachment · Scanned by Gmail

FIGURE 12.7 K Email Correspondence

I was told that they were going to reapply and wait another five months to find out. Until then, they were going to focus on the core game production but put the audio on hold until they got full funding and would keep me posted. I replied with understanding and requested if they could pay the other half of the amount that was in the agreement that they signed.

to me

Hi Chase,

We've hit a little funding hiccup – we didn't get the grant that we were hoping for and we will have to reapply and wait another 5 months to find out, so we're going to have to focus on the core game production and put the audio on hold until we get our full funding.

Sorry for that. I hope you'll still be available when the time comes, but I totally understand if you have to move on in the meantime, but please keep me posted!

Talk soon,

FIGURE 12.8 K Email Correspondence

"K" said that they didn't have the adequate funding to pay the final invoice at the present time and their excuse was that since the work that I've done was only a couple of passes, they felt what they paid me was fair.

Chase Bethea

Hi

Oh wow. Okay. I'm sorry to hear that. I hope everything comes around for the re-application. Thank you for telling me know.

Do I still get the $1500 per our agreement for the $3,000 amount to be caught up for June at least? Or is that not possible right now?

I'd still like to work on the project if your funding comes through.

Thank you kindly,

Chase

FIGURE 12.9 K Email Correspondence

I replied respectfully that if they wanted to work together in the future, what was fair was to honour the agreed contract that they drafted and that in the contract, there was nothing that stated theme passes to equate the amount of work done.

Hi Chase

Unfortunately we don't have adequate funding to pay that final invoice at present, but I also feel that given that we only did a couple of passes on the intro theme so far that $1500 US is probably fair payment for that. Let me know if you feel otherwise and I'll se what we can do.

I do hope you're still available and that we can get back together once we have our funding in place – either through the grant or investment. I'll certainly keep you posted on our progress!

FIGURE 12.10 K Email Correspondence

Basically, there was nothing in the contract or in the Exhibits to justify what he thought he paid for in terms of the work that I had done. I also requested a proper milestone audio asset list to justify assets for the fee.

In the same month, I requested to use the video with my music for a reel. My email was never answered.

Chase Bethea

Hi

Okay I understand if you do not have the adequate funding at the moment then you do not have it.

With all due respect however, if you wish to work together in the future with me, please keep in mind I believe it is only fair to honor the fee agreed upon in our contract. I do not recall it saying in the contract what milestone work for the audio was needed in order to validate my contractor fee. If I missed that please let me know.

In the future, I would like a proper milestone or audio asset list so that you can receive appropriate assets needed to justify my fee, if that is your concern. I have no problem delivering what you need and I am always happy to make any adjustments necessary.

I am passionate about the project and I would still love to work on it so please reach out when you are ready. I'll be following any details on YouTube and Twitter.

Thank you again

Kind Wishes
Chase

FIGURE 12.11 K Email Correspondence

I reached out in October of the same year to inquire about the project. By following the updates they were posting, I discovered that they hired a different composer, so I emailed again and asked about it.

Chase Bethea

Hi

I hope all is well with you and production.

I was wondering if you wanted the SFX soundscape I made for the concept you gave me about the ship?

In addition, I was also hoping to get your permission to post this video I made from the web-comic "Left Behind" for my reel? Please let me know your thoughts at your earliest convenience. Thank you!

Kind Regards,
Chase

FIGURE 12.12 K Email Correspondence

Finally, I received a reply, stating that the development was going great, even though funding was low, but they still found money to pay a "young composer" from their region. "K" stated that they wished cost was not a factor, but it was a major factor and that the new composer was a third of the cost. "K" also said, "I want to be clear we did not have any problem with the rates. We simply couldn't afford them without the long-term funding securely in place."

Chase Bethea

Hey

I hope all is well with you. How is the project going? I just saw the concept post with the music. Looks good! Did you happen to hire a different composer?

Also, I was wondering if you received my previous email a couple months back about the video I did for the audition and your approval to use it for my reel?

At your earliest convenience, please let me know!

Kind Regards,
Chase

FIGURE 12.13 K Email Correspondence

I replied with the disappointment of them, hiring another composer and them not working with me if cost was not the factor. In addition, the ball was in their court to negotiate what would've been flexible to meet their budget. Do you see the contradiction here? When given the rate and they see what I charge, can they determine if they can afford it? If not, what can I share or I can ask what they can afford? I also requested since they had found the money to pay a third of the cost to the new composer and that they had no problem with my rate that they honour the contract that they drafted and signed to pay the remaining amount owed or I was going to seek legal action. I found it to be very unfair and unprofessional. Luckily, I asked for half of the amount upfront.

to me

Hey Chase,

Thanks for checking in! How are things going for you? Are you working on anything exciting right now?

The game development is going great, and it's really starting to take shape, particularly the whole character psychology side of things.

Unfortunately we're still living hand to mouth as relates to funding. We're hoping to get on that government loan program around Christmas time, but it is highly competitive, so we don't know what our chances are at present.

We've just started working with a young composer from Toronto who we met at our last show. I really wish we were in a position where cost was not a factor in this process, but the sad fact is that it is a major factor for us right now. He's been working for us for about 1/3 of your original cost, so we are able to limp along. I want to be clear – we did not have any problem with your rates, we simply couldn't afford them without long term funding securely in place.

As for the video, I'm not sure I recall that – I remember the audio samples you prepared, but not the video. Can you refresh my memory – did you do a video with the comic pages in it?

At any rate, with all the samples, you're more than welcome to use them for your reel. Please refer to them as 'audio proposals for , or 'proposed audio for etc.

All the best!

FIGURE 12.14 K Email Correspondence

He replied, "Wow Chase. That's a bad look."

He stated that they pay all contractors who deliver work and go into the game that my work was not accepted, never used or released and did not match their expectations. The truth finally comes out here. "K" said,

> Had we not found our funding crisis we would've terminated the contract anyway, but felt the funding issue was a gentler option for parting ways. Asking for full payment for work that was never used is pretty rich. We felt we were meeting you halfway by paying you for the time we feel the work was delivered.

Chase Bethea

Hey

Things are good. Yes, I'm scoring and doing sound design for a game that has about 2.5 million plays and was at PAX Indie MegaBooth.

I'm happy to hear that game development is going great on your end. Wonderful news

Sorry to hear about the funding situation. I hope you get it

Thank you for the clearance on the sample work for future reel purposes

In regards, to the composer, I will be upfront and honest to say I am disappointed that you did not at least offer me the rate that worked for you before signing the contract. We could have also worked out a deals that would have worked for you and I could have stayed on the project. It was in your court to negotiate and I would have been flexible to meet your budget

Since you have the budget to pay someone a 1/3 of the cost of my rate and since you stated that you had no problem with my rate, I am going to have to ask that you please pay me the remaining $1500 owed to me for the services I did earlier this year ASAP. If you do not, I'm going to seek legal action immediately. I find this very unfair and unprofessional to not have paid me what you signed a contract on. I know how funding goes but the professional action to do is to pay your contractors for services rendered and due to the contract I was not compensated in full

I hope we can keep this as cordial as possible and resolve this swiftly. Thank you!

Regards
Chase

FIGURE 12.15 K Email Correspondence

I replied that the "bad look" was that it was never stated or outlined in the contract what work was approved or accepted, and he never said that he did not like the work. In addition, he did not have an asset list for me to work from. In the signed contract, they did not have any deadlines exhibited. I continued to explain that I tried to communicate with him on multiple accounts as best as I could to understand what he needed, and it was his responsibility to lay out and properly document coursework for me to achieve the requested services.

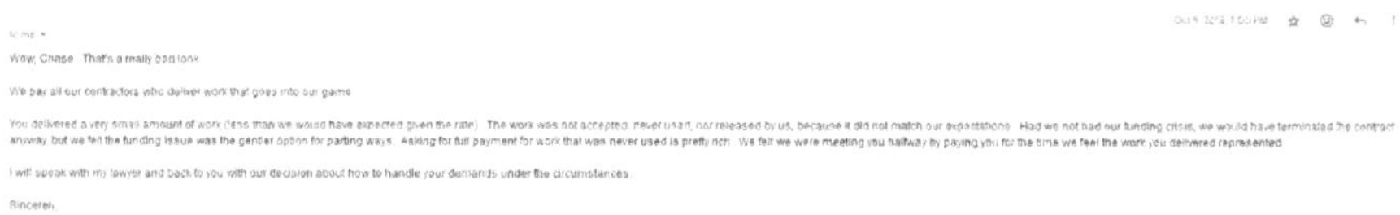

to me

Wow, Chase. That's a really bad look.

We pay all our contractors who deliver work that goes into our game

You delivered a very small amount of work (less than we would have expected given the rate). The work was not accepted, never used, nor released by us, because it did not match our expectations. Had we not had our funding crisis, we would have terminated the contract anyway, but we felt the funding issue was the gentler option for parting ways. Asking for full payment for work that was never used is pretty rich. We felt we were meeting you halfway by paying you for the time we feel the work you delivered represented.

I will speak with my lawyer and back to you with our decision about how to handle your demands under the circumstances.

Sincerely

FIGURE 12.16 K Email Correspondence

Chase Bethea

A bad look is you never stating in the contract, what work was approved or accepted. You never said you did not like the work I sent. You did not even have a asset list for me to work off of stating deadlines of how much work would be expected of me. This is not in the contract that you signed! In addition, I tried to communicate with you on multiple accounts as best as I could to understand what you needed. It was your responsibility to lay out proper documented course work for me to achieve for services rendered by certain dates. Simple

So, you're upset because I'm asking what is fair, professional and in the contract? If you simply said "Hey this isn't working out, we aren't happy with your work this will be your final payment." None of that was said by you.

Thanks

Chase

FIGURE 12.17 K Email Correspondence

So, in all, it seems like they were upset because I was asking for what was fair, professional and in the contract? If they did not like the work, they simply could've said, "This isn't working out. We are not happy with the work you have been sending, and this will be your final payment." None of that was said to me and I was never paid the outstanding amount. Unfortunately, I waited too long to seek a lawyer to move in the proper legal format and this was a very costly learning lesson.

This situation impacted me greatly and was a massive learning experience for me. It affected my life mentally and financially as I was counting on the rate that "K" agreed to pay me in the signed contract and in which he cowardly backed out of. I had to resort to getting a full-time, retail job for a year to make ends meet. It was very disheartening and stressful, but I had to do what I had to do to survive. If this had gone differently, in a copacetic, professional, mature manner, I believe this would have been a project that could have possibly launched my career sooner. One of the reasons being that they had proper marketing ideas and videos to promote everyone on the team.

12.3 THE UNPLEASANT POTION

A game that didn't ship. Not a bad experience, just an experience.

It was in February 2020 that I got recommended to write the music for this game. I remember being very excited. I had a virtual call with the team. There were several of them, including the producer. After the initial

FIGURE 12.18 PAX East 2020 – Escalator Descent

call, I wrote a small demo which the entire team loved. They said they would get back to me soon. I recall coming down the escalator at my first PAX (PAX East) when I received the email from the studio, offering me the position to write the music for the game. Pure joy and glee overcame me. I've finally been accepted by a big-name studio.

The process of working in this game was an absolute delight. The team was great, from the CEO and producer to the artists, writers and programmers. They were all supportive. They were helpful and personable. Although we navigated collaboration at the beginning of lockdown during the pandemic, spirits were still strong and vibrant. I could tell the team was built very well and it was a dream come true to be able to work together with these personalities. This is a rarity in game development.

Because of this, my creativity was able to flourish and flow effortlessly. In the moments of problem-solving middleware workflows that I was unfamiliar with, I operated with confidence and prevailed. The support from the team was so powerful that it boosted my productivity to the point where I was ahead of schedule.

In one meeting, I was presenting the third track that I had finished for the game. Several team members, including the producer, gave their feedback. Typically, the meeting would end after that, but I had a surprise for them. I had already finished writing the fourth track and presented it to them as well. The team was shocked by my efficiency as well as pleased by the piece of music I composed. It goes to show that when you're respected, properly compensated and appreciated, how much a person's performance can shine.

I completed the final tracks and sadly my collaboration time ended with them. I was hoping to be brought on in-house to score more of their game titles but alas I was not. I withheld final hope of at least releasing a soundtrack of the game to have my work be heard by the world.

After waiting two years since scoring a great game in five months and tracking down the CEO of the company for a year, I found out some unfortunate news on May 10, 2022:

> Unfortunately, we will not be launching the game in a full launch. We have a small games team, and we are swamped with managing our two live apps. It is a bummer as I know the team put a lot of sweat and equity behind 'the unpleasant potion'. Sorry for the bad news.

This sucked big time. Not only was this a game I was excited for, but the studio was one of the bigger game studios in Los Angeles. I was recommended to the producer by a friend I met at GDC years ago, who worked there as a narrative writer. My previous bids were rejected by other game studios, and this was the first bid I won. It was my introduction to audio middleware that wasn't so popular. Once the game launched, I had planned to use this as a boost to get bigger gigs that paid better. I wanted to release a soundtrack, a physical vinyl copy, and perform my work live at gaming concerts/conventions. Now that no one will see the game, it has left me in an unmovable position. Forcing me to pivot once again.

12.4 ABOUT FACE GAMES

I interviewed for a game company in Burbank that I was recommended by an industry colleague for the position of video game composer.

When I was waiting in the lobby area for the first interview, a gentleman looked at me and walked past me. He did not greet me.

It wasn't until I had the second interview that I discerned he was the owner of the company. This is another "flag on the play." It's not the best look if he is "the face of the company." I thought to myself, is this the dynamic and culture of the company that I am walking into?

After the second interview, I felt hesitant about it. I recall my father saying, "Isn't that what you wanted? You wanted to be a video game composer."

Some people may be thinking you could be looking a gift horse in the mouth because I sabotaged the last interview. The owner and the previous interviewer asked me the exact same questions twice. They could have been doing it to test me to see if my answers were consistent or they were not communicating with each other between the interviews. If it was the latter, which I believe it was, this was a red flag to me because if there were no communication with each other at this level, I knew once I started working with them, communication gaps would ensue and that's never good when deadlines have to be met. This is important. However, that second interview did not feel like one. It felt like a police investigation.

So, I did not think this was looking a gift horse in the mouth. It was me recognising my value and not subjecting myself to whatever games I believe they were trying to play with me.

12.5 MILES BEHIND

I found this game on X (Twitter). I reached out to the developer. I managed to get a meeting with him, and we had a virtual call in 2021. Initially, the conversation started well. The developer expressed interest in terms of integrating music. I went as far as to make a couple of demos, to show how the adaptive music really enhanced the experience of the game. In addition, I included the audio middleware presentation to show my excitement and continued interest.

We discussed audio middleware integration possibilities, negotiated with the audio middleware company and tried to work something out with music licenses due to his budget. The call went well.

With the developer working on the game in the late hours of the night, we wrapped up the conversation and agreed to keep in touch. This is exactly what I did.

I sent multiple emails to him following up to see how development was going from March 2021 to April 22, 2022. No response. Now, to his credit, he did respond once or twice.

However, my thoughts are that if he did not want to work on the game with me or if he was not interested in continuing the conversation about having me compose the soundtrack for the game, then all he had to do was say so.

It's highly disappointing to think that people can do this to others. Not responding is never okay and extremely rude. Of course, there are some exceptions such as family member bereavement and other unexpected life events. However, there was some kind of correspondence in the beginning, and some follow-up emails and the last correspondence was on good terms, then what's the issue?

If it were me, I would not engage in collaboration conversations until I have the bandwidth and I would express that if someone reached out. I know I need to respond accordingly.

Here are some suggestions on how to respond in these situations. A simple email or a message saying, "I'm no longer interested." Another response could be "I'm sorry to tell you, I found someone else to work with" or "I am going a different route with the music. I hope that you can understand. Thank you." By not responding, you are creating animosity, and you could be creating enemies. Even when I talked with a 30-year game developer industry veteran about this, he said, "If you do not reply, it messes with mindsets. By saying 'No' it tells us where we stand."

Some people have the mentality of "you don't owe anybody anything" but the courtesy of a reply, I feel, is deserved as a human being. In this industry, I have found that some people seem to have this attitude that we're not owed a response especially when there was a connection that was made initially. But they don't seem to realise that by ignoring the connection response, it does something to the mental psyche. It shortens the longevity of working in the industry which is supposed to be a collaborative activity. It is also supposed to be a business. Unfortunately, I have met many people in this industry over the past decade who seem to not have the emotional aptitude to be courteous and just respond in a kind manner. This is part of rejection.

The industry is flawed in many ways. The key problem I continuously see and that I find very frustrating is that people who operate in this space act immature and ignorant with basic communication skills. We wonder why we don't get things done. We wonder why there are so many lay-offs. We wonder why games get delayed. We wonder why a lot of things about our industry are because of little actions like these that build up to something more. If we pause or stop, and take the time to sit back and say, "I know I'm busy. I know I can't respond right now, but I should at least make the effort to say that I acknowledge the outreach and apologies in advance for late replies or I am not interested." It does not have to be a dissertation reply. Let's get something done. It's really simple but I guess the mindset has to be there.

12.6 THE AGENT M FILES

In 2015, there was a new PR agent who wanted to represent composers in games. He was from another country, so English was not his first language. Let's call him "Agent M". There was a post about him looking for new clients to represent. In this case, it was another dream come true feeling. This PR was different. They were going to do PR to maintain the image of the composer and find work for them too. They were also going to attend global trades such as GDC (Game Developer Conference), E3 (at the time it was present), Gamescom, Tokyo Game Show and more. This was a massive win as I was mostly unable to attend some of these international game conferences. They were going to pitch to potential clients, set up meetings and interviews so that the composer could focus on writing, other matters and family. Again, a dream partnership I had been wanting for some years for someone in the game at my level. Someone who understood how to build with someone in their career and their costs was affordable (mostly because they did not live in the United States). They offered a three-month trial period with an affordable rate. So, I hired them for that rate. And so, you know how the story goes by now.

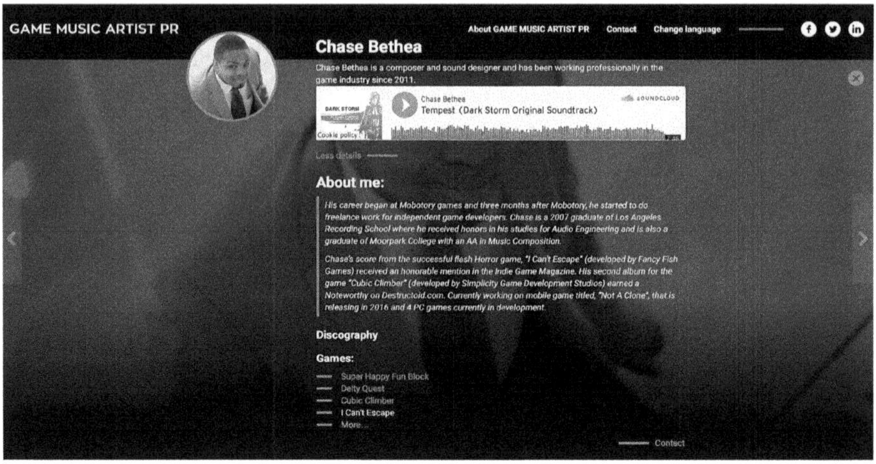

FIGURE 12.19 Game Music Artist PR Page

After we sorted out the details of the contract, the collaboration started off well. He got right to work. He set up my artist page on the PR website and began searching for interviews for me to do and was very responsive. Agent M would send me job postings for audio designer and audio internships at AAA companies. These were the jobs I was able to find with a quick Google search, but he also sent jobs that were not in my state or several hours away from where I resided. He seemed to think that if I applied, they would save my contact information and reach out to me. I can assure you here and now that to this day, this has *never* happened. Automated replies exist more now than in 2016 and I did not even receive one of those. From what I used to hear from HR, Audio Directors and hiring managers from many studios is to "read the job description. Do not apply if you are not in the same municipality." If I recall correctly, this is because these studios cannot afford to relocate the candidate to the city at their expense (Even though these companies make billions of dollars annually, that is another conversation entirely). So, their point is if you apply and you are not in the location specified to come in to work on campus, they will ignore and/or delete your application. I know these companies have HR systems that filter through applications that do not have the right keywords, so your chances of someone contacting you at all are slim to none, especially if your location is not close by. So, I would be wasting my time doing so and I felt he was wasting his time and my money by sending me lists of job postings that were irrelevant.

With some redirection, he was able to pitch my music to some Japanese developer companies and a few indie game propositions. However, he was only able to get me interviews and amplify the media I was already posting. He did his best for the three months I contracted him.

Some years passed and Agent M reached out to me at the beginning of 2020, requesting to work as my manager and what I would expect. I exclaimed my enthusiasm to work as my manager would be great, and I would expect the following. 1. For him to find *only* paying game project gigs that will be worth my time and his, so that he can receive a proper percentage too. 2. For him to help me negotiate proper compensation and set up contracts with developers, so that I can focus on making the music for the project. 3. For us to have at least a weekly or biweekly check-in with each other. 4. For him to help me book game concerts to perform my music worldwide. I expressed that my goal at the time was to reach AAA composer status, and I would be happy even if I was working on bigger indie projects as long as I'm working. I was ready to send new demos and music that were unreleased that I believe should have landed me that work. I shared with him that I want to succeed in this industry long term. I asked him to let me know his thoughts and what he would expect from me.

Agent M took several weeks to review my requests before replying, and when he did, he replied with a semi-increased request amount. Now, to be clear, I had no problem paying this if I knew he was going to search for jobs that it would make sense to cover his fee with. I knew he was capable of finding these gigs because another composer he was representing for some time and their career had grown. The link between them though was that they were from the same country.

I had explained some points to Agent M. First, I was a little concerned that his response took seven weeks and he wavered too long. I expressed that I knew that we were both busy, however, the time it takes him to respond to me and discuss was not acceptable for me. Keep in mind, this was someone who replied to me consistently before even when he was at a New Year's party. I understand boundaries become established or change but I still consider a check-in during those weeks to be professional. For me, the responsiveness showed how much I was or was not a priority. If I'm counting on work to live and this person has my "livelihood" partially in their hands based on gigs he lands for me, I would expect to hear from them frequently and often. By him not responding for seven weeks was a "Toledo bull".

I went on to share that I thought that he might consider the new collaboration as a "trade of services", especially considering he requested me to take time to write articles for his game music website and podcast reviews of games. This was something that also required work, my time and I was not compensated for.

In addition to the trade of services, I offered for him to receive 10% of any game project he finds, negotiates and lands in turn for his work and effort. For example, if he were to land me a game gig where I got paid US$10,000 to write the music, he would get paid $1,000 of that. That is substantially larger than the semi-nominal fee he was asking per month. If he was to acquire that type of gig that month for me, he would make that US$1,000 in one month rather than four months. I conveyed that this is how some top agents who represent AAA composers in games in the United States work. I apologised for not making the offer clearer and/or if I misunderstood his initial collaboration proposal and I understood if the work was too much for him and that he could back out. Unfortunately, I could not agree to his request to pay him monthly and recounted that I need to find bigger work projects in order for the collaboration to properly work.

The reply he wrote was cordial. He thanked me for my honesty and said that everything I wrote was valuable information for him. He expressed that my job requests require a large amount of time and dedication and that we will need to build my brand. However, he understood my arguments.

He continued that at the time he was working on two AAA games, so he knew the numbers that I shared in my example.

He asked me to think about whether I wanted him to just look for jobs for me because then, he will not charge any monthly fee except if he procures a gig, he will request 15%. However, if I wanted him to only do promotion for me in addition to searching for the gigs, then he wanted me to think about how much I could pay him monthly for such work in addition to giving 10% for any game contracts signed. Things are getting interesting. One thing I appreciated about Agent M is that he was able to negotiate.

Lastly, he did thank me for the contribution to the articles and that he hoped that he would be able to pay me soon.

After some brief reflection, I replied the same day, mentioning that I would like him to look for those jobs that pay. I also expressed that I would agree to the 15% once the contract was signed, and an upfront amount has been transferred. I was already handling promotion, so I did not need help there.

Agent M recounted that 15% only works if I got the gig and if I wanted him to deal with the production of music, project care and searching for orchestras, orchestrators, vocalists, etc., then his fee may increase to 20% because usually working on such productions lasts from two to three years.

Okay, here we go. More surprise information. I am unsure why this was not said initially. Nonetheless, it was said before new contracts were signed. I recapped that I thoroughly understood the conditions and that we were in concurrence. I shared that if I needed orchestras, ensembles, etc., I would consult him first as I had some connections on my end that I could reach out to. I requested all the talking points be in a contract before any work began.

I also inquired if he truly had the time for it to begin so soon, since he mentioned he was in the middle of two AAA game productions. My concern was that it took him seven weeks to respond, and I did not want to be left hanging in the wind again.

To my immediate surprise, he responded with a potential gig to demo for a game. Unfortunately, this is where it falls apart.

Keep in mind there is a time difference. They are in another country. I was asked if I had time to compose demo music over the weekend. If the developers liked it, I would get a commission to compose the music for the game. I replied the same day that I was available to write the demo and thanked him. I also requested to have more details and if we could get the contract in order too. Agent M replied that he would send me the answers the next day.

Tick. Tock. Saturday at 3:40 PM PST, he answered my questions. He shared that it is a new studio in Europe, and it will be their first game. For a minute of composed music, they will pay US$300. He mentioned that for now it is a contest/pitch, if I won it, they would pay me for the demo and employ me to compose music for the full game. However, now the details change. Agent M asks if I had time to indite music for a two-minute trailer by Monday. So, do I not get paid for the other minute of music?

I thanked him for the information but expressed my confusion about some things that were still unclear to me. I asked if it was a minute of music or two minutes of music for the contest/pitch and if the contest would end Monday or start Monday?

Agent M replies on Sunday! He does not clearly answer my questions. All he said was if I get the gig, they will pay me $300 for a minute of composed music, and the contest/pitch ends on Tuesday. Finally, he sent the brief as well. Although, calling it a brief is funny. It was quite long and detailed.

Since the brief was sent late, I exclaimed I will send the demo by Tuesday. I worked on it for hours all day Monday and Tuesday and kept the correspondence fluid. I emailed him Monday saying I will deliver the demo considering I did not get all the information at the point at which I was asked (Friday) and our time zone differences.

He acknowledged my email and said they will await my submission.

I sent the demo on Tuesday and this was his response. "Thanks, I know that this is a demo, but its quality is very poor. If I can advise you something, change the sample library or equipment, otherwise you will not get bigger productions. Such friendly advice."

I was in shock. I really did not know what to say to him. Well, I did know what I wanted to say. The first thing was, "Excuse me?" However, since English was not their first language, I kept my emotions in check. So, my only reply was "Wow. Thank you."

By the following Saturday, this was the reply,

> I hope you had a great week? Unfortunately, I was afraid of this, your demo was of very poor quality and the developers did not notice the potential for cooperation in it. Therefore, if I am to keep looking for jobs for you, you have to do something about it. In addition, I need your showreel to show the next developer team what you can do. Have a great weekend and stay safe!

The email was cordial, but I have to admit my ego was hurt. I went to audio engineering school. I was mentored by AAA composers and I followed and studied many AAA composers' work very closely. I used high production samples not soundfonts (no disrespect to soundfonts, I still think they are cool for the right application), but my point is how could they say my demo was "very poor quality". They gave me a day to do it and yes most can do that work in a day but to follow the brief in major detail that they wanted with an orchestral score for $300 only to degrade it without one compliment, I found to be disrespectful. I know that people say, "do not take it personally" but I did, and it was hard. It was an unfair advantage. In hindsight, I should have had the perspicacity to say "No" to writing the demo. When offered to pitch, there is always a choice. No one made me do it.

Since I had time to think about the response, I replied, "After deep consideration, I have decided that we should end the collaboration. Thank you for your effort. Have a good weekend." Agent M replied,

> Of course I understand and forgive [me] if I have offended you in some way, but I prefer to be honest with you than to promise the golden mountains, I hope you will understand that? If will it be possible to send you demos of other composers so that you can compare the level.

I expressed that I appreciated the honesty and understood greatly. However, I deeply felt our communication had not been the best for some time and it had made things more difficult on my end. It had made me unhappy and frustrated.

I continued to verbalise that I had already sent my demos/music to my composer friends, many of whom were AAA composers who worked on games such as *God of War, PlanetSide 2* and *Burnout*. In addition, I had been listed in a couple of sample libraries, one of which was owned by an AAA composer.

I shared that he did offend me but not by what he said but by how he said it and reiterated that this is a communication issue. I thanked him for the opportunity and his effort and wished him all the best.

Agent M's response was that he also thought that there was a lack of understanding and misunderstanding in our communication. He conveyed that it was not his goal to offend me and congratulated me on all that I achieved. He recommended for us to "relax from each other," return to the topic of cooperation in a few months and discuss our expectations. He wished me the best as well and that was it.

Very cordial. I have respect for his response. He apologised, explained his intentions and even with my emotions being heavy upon me, I still was diplomatic and as professional as I could be too.

Lots of lessons learned here. The first one is to be clear about communication. Outline the expectations early and do not rush into things.

Hmm . . . this sounds like dating, but the lessons are applicable. This way, neither party can come back later confused or upset claiming something was not communicated properly.

Second, you do not have to pitch if it doesn't feel right. I do not condone crunch. I am not that type of creator. I work well under certain pressure but not tight pressure. I do not believe in the constant tight pressure the industry puts on humans. I believe it is disgusting. Therefore, I should not have participated but I was impressed by the opportunity Agent M had found so quickly and I felt I was in the position to prove to myself that I could do it as well as to him. I forgot about my morales, and it suffered. I will be transpicuous and say the demo was not the best. The mix suffered but I do not concur with Agent M that it was "poor quality".

The third lesson is to be prepared to walk away from something that isn't working. There does not have to be bad blood between the parties but if the work ethic and communication do not meet your standards, as much as it sucks, just break ties. In the present, the deeper and inner you will be at peace even when you mentally are not there yet.

Even though I dealt with communication expectations and lack of responses from potential clients, I can only surmise that music or my music specifically was not important enough to them nor was some form of brief correspondence professionalism. The good thing about this industry is that there is a decent percentage that do operate on the level of correspondence professionalism that value music for their project. They see it as part of the development not an "add-on".

I no longer take it personally and this took a lot of years for me to get to that place mentally. Their actions had nothing to do with me. I just remember when they didn't respond to that email, or they "ghosted" me they have to live with that guilt, that unprofessionalism, that lack of integrity and themselves longer than anyone else.

We shouldn't promise people things we can't pull through on. Even though the "world doesn't owe us anything". This statement may be factual to some people. Nonetheless, it does something to the mental psyche when someone is ignored. I think and suggest one should at least owe it to themself to be a person of their word. I still believe one should have some kind of professional and human etiquette to respond to people if they have been courteous to you.

I think most of us need to do better about keeping up with each other and reaching out not only when we need something. I think most of us need to do better about replying sooner to the ones closest to us. I think and suggest most of us need to do better about setting reminders. I truly believe most of us need to do better about not taking things out of context or personal all of the time, especially when someone is trying to help. Most of us need to do better about saying "thank you" sooner to the person we sought help from. I definitely believe people should not downplay someone else's success. I think the majority of us need to do better about not assuming. We can do better about genuinely caring. I strongly believe the majority need to do better about taking responsibility and accountability when someone is wrong. Most of us can do better about not making excuses and respecting each other's time. The majority can do better about being honest. The majority can do better about uplifting and sharing each other's work and success without having to ask. The world doesn't have to owe us anything if we just practice better habits with ourselves. If we did that, I believe the people in the world could instantly and naturally benefit from a better quality of life.

This industry seems to pride itself on professionalism but does not practice it in the moments that it truly counts. I sense that laziness slides in somewhere and deters the perpetual motion of proper enactment. Maybe the intention is there but the effort falls short and then the industry wonders why there is so much drama. Do not get me wrong, every industry has its flaws, but it cannot constantly straddle the fence. Is it going to be consistent and honest with professionalism on all fronts or is it going to continually be nonchalant, suffer in silence and act surprised when the bullshit occurs? My deepest hope is that the industry gets its act together, cleans up its mess, learns from the mistakes and does not repeat them so that we can all level up and advance in a healthy way together.

I am sharing these anecdotes to show the grind it took to get here the past ten years but as Clinton Sparks said, "Most overnight success takes 10 years to create but most overnight success doesn't last 10 years." It's probably because of burnout, anxiety and other factors. Initially, I thought and made a plan to achieve the majority of my goals in five years but that was not what happened. People have perceived me as being successful in many forms, I am Googleable, I do a lot of guest speaking and I am a live performer. I wonder if they ever think of the many steps I took to become

Googleable. The mindset and approach I practice to do guest speaking. How I took a speech class in Moorpark College way before I decided to be a game composer and why I pivoted to performing. Most people just say the phrases, but do not consider the practice and conservative execution of the mini goals. They just see the minutes of the moments. That's okay. This is why I wrote this book so that I could show people the inside of what goes on, the mental tools used to paint the picture they see once it has been done.

CHAPTER 13

Do a Barrel Roll! – Not a Sneak Roll!

I was reaching out to a potential client to inquire about doing work for a game. I did a music demo for them, and they were excited about what I wrote. It turned from inquiring about music to being asked about doing sound design, assisting with onboarding other composers who were selected and checking another audio person's work to finally requesting dialogue editing for three languages. In addition, I already offered to do audio implementation. He tried what I call a "sneak roll". It's when a client or company inquires to hire or hires you and then sneakily tries to add on more roles that are in the "vicinity" of the main role. In this example, music-making is one job and not directly related to sound design. Sound design is not related to overseeing another audio team member's work. That's typically an Audio Lead position. Audio Leads normally do not do all the dialogue editing, especially in three languages. At this point, we are crossing the threshold of localisation.

My point is that not all audio roles are created equal. There are different skill sets and salary brackets that come with it. Is it possible to do it all? Yes. For an indie game with very little budget. "Abso-fucking-lutley not!" When I told him this is not how the conversation started and the position he really wanted turned into an audio director, in the end, the guy had the audacity and insouciance to tell me "No! It doesn't matter that it's AA or indie, the work is the work!" It's a lot of roles he tried to sneak roll me for. You can see in this correspondence that I outlined this.

DOI: 10.1201/9781003422815-13

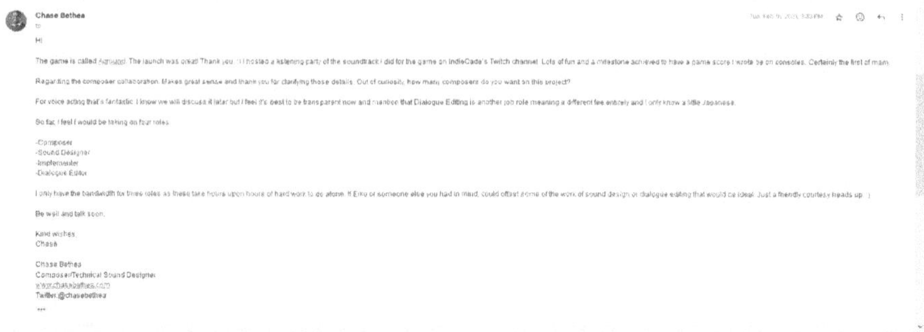

Chase Bethea

to

Hi

The game is called [illegible]. The launch was great! Thank you :) I hosted a listening party of the soundtrack I did for the game on IndieCade's Twitch channel. Lots of fun and a milestone achieved to have a game score I wrote be on consoles. Certainly the first of many.

Regarding the composer collaboration. Makes great sense and thank you for clarifying those details. Out of curiosity, how many composers do you want on this project?

For voice acting that's fantastic. I know we will discuss it later but I feel it's best to be transparent now and mention that Dialogue Editing is another job role meaning a different fee entirely and I only know a little Japanese.

So far, I feel I would be taking on four roles.

-Composer
-Sound Designer
-Implementer
-Dialogue Editor

I only have the bandwidth for three roles as these take hours upon hours of hard work to do alone. If Eiko or someone else you had in mind, could offset some of the work of sound design or dialogue editing that would [illegible] ideal. Just a friendly courtesy heads up :)

Be well and talk soon,

Kind wishes,
Chase

Chase Bethea
Composer/Technical Sound Designer
www.chasebethea.com
Twitter: @chasebethea

FIGURE 13.1 Do a Barrel Roll Not a Sneak Roll

Editing dialogues in a different language is the job of localisation. How am I supposed to know two languages and edit them if I don't speak those languages? How could I know when the sentences end? How did he expect this to happen? Did he expect me to learn the languages? If so, that's a big ask and based on his mentality, I do not think he would be willing to pay me additionally to learn the languages either. I wonder if he truly thought it through.

His argument was that localisation is only an AAA service. Not true. I worked on a few games that received localisation and these small game studios are definitely not AAA.

He continued to try to put words in my mouth by saying, "He didn't ask me to cast voice actors." Correct but he did ask if I could work with other composers and oversee their work. That is the role of an Audio Lead or Audio Director with the responsibilities of possibly writing music and overseeing the entire audio team and workflows. An Audio Programmer, Audio Implementer, Sound Designer, Music Composer and a Dialogue Editor are all different jobs. That's five jobs and I don't think as an independent developer that it is fair to ask one person to do all those things unless you're going to be properly compensated for it. If that's the case, an Audio Director job with those responsibilities would be getting paid closer to $100,000. I know an independent developer is not going to be able to afford that. For this to be fair, I would request to take a huge revenue share, of all gross sales, not net, to make up for that amount. I would be willing to guess that what they were going to offer was not even close to 100k. My hypothesis is that they probably were going to offer me minimum wage based on whatever they can afford. I estimate the offer to be between $13.00 and $15.00 an hour for lots of hours of work. There needs to be a lot of funding considered to match that type of responsibility.

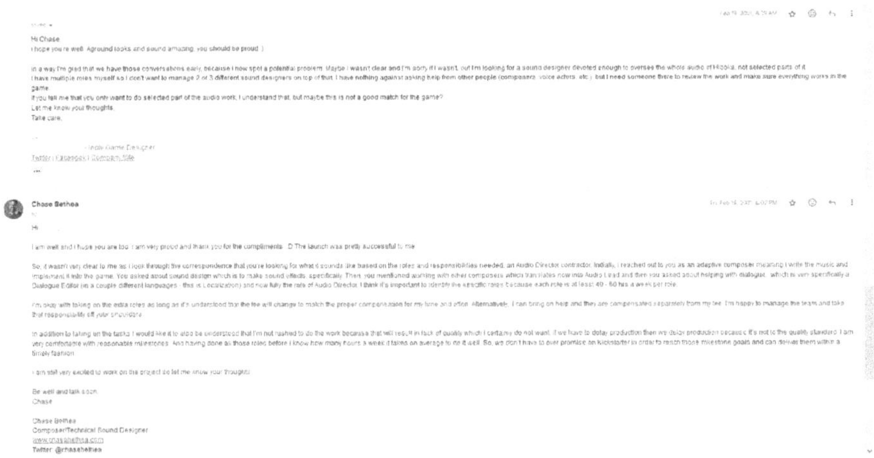

Hi Chase
I hope you're well. Aground looks and sound amazing, you should be proud :)

In a way I'm glad that we have those conversations early, because I now spot a potential problem. Maybe I wasn't clear and I'm sorry if I wasn't, but I'm looking for a sound designer devoted enough to oversee the whole audio of Hibika, not selected parts of it.
I have multiple roles myself so I don't want to manage 2 or 3 different sound designers on top of that. I have nothing against asking help from other people (composers, voice actors, etc.) but I need someone there to review the work and make sure everything works in the game.
If you tell me that you only want to do selected part of the audio work, I understand that, but maybe this is not a good match for the game?
Let me know your thoughts.
Take care,

– Indie Game Designer
Twitter | Facebook | Company Site

Chase Bethea

Hi

I am well and I hope you are too. I am very proud and thank you for the compliments :D The launch was pretty successful to me.

So, it wasn't very clear to me as I look through the correspondence that you're looking for what it sounds like based on the roles and responsibilities needed, an Audio Director contractor. Initially, I reached out to you as an adaptive composer meaning I write the music and implement it into the game. You asked about sound design which is to make sound effects, specifically. Then, you mentioned working with other composers which translates now into Audio Lead and then you asked about helping with dialogue, which is very specifically a Dialogue Editor (in a couple different languages - this is Localization) and now fully the role of Audio Director. I think it's important to identify the specific roles because each role is at least 40 - 60 hrs a week per role.

I'm okay with taking on the extra roles as long as it's understood that the fee will change to match the proper compensation for my time and effort. Alternatively, I can bring on help and they are compensated separately from my fee. I'm happy to manage the team and take that responsibility off your shoulders.

In addition to taking on the tasks I would like it to also be understood that I'm not rushed to do the work because that will result in lack of quality which I certainly do not want. If we have to delay production then we delay production because it's not to the quality standard. I am very comfortable with reasonable milestones. And having done all those roles before I know how many hours a week it takes on average to do it well. So, we don't have to over promise on Kickstarter in order to reach those milestone goals and can deliver them within a timely fashion.

I am still very excited to work on the project so let me know your thoughts.

Be well and talk soon,
Chase

Chase Bethea
Composer/Technical Sound Designer
www.chasebethea.com
Twitter: @chasebethea

FIGURE 13.2 Do a Barrel Roll Not a Sneak Roll

It's apparent that the homework was not done and there was an unclear sense of what each role truly entails to understand the amount of work it takes to do per role. Only then, I believe, he would understand more how much work it really is.

I also think it's unfair not to be able to mention these experiences publicly. We don't have to say the names of these companies and if they find out that we are talking about it, the blame still falls on them. They are the ones who are trying to squeeze so much work out of us and take advantage of us. It's not cool, it's not fair and it's not right. I'm not going to sit by that for anything.

Here is a parallel example. If you're talking to someone that you've been interested in for a long time and you're thinking that maybe the relationship is going to work. However, a red flag comes along, and they say, "Well, if we get together, you have to be comfortable with XYZ." Maybe X is, they are interested in having an open relationship. Y is they pass gas a lot or they are on their phone a bunch. If that doesn't work for you, then it's not a good fit because you shouldn't have to adapt your principles just to be with that person even if it seems like that person is beautiful as hell. There may be a possibility that you will feel great with them, and they might enhance your life in some way. There will always be a "what if" factor. However, you can most likely tell within your own personality if it's not going to work for you. Most of the time, if you've been living your life a certain way, then why would you adapt under those preconditions for the possibility that it will work out? When it clicks, it should work out under the conditions that fit best for both people.

It's kind of unfortunate that we have to shut up and not talk about these matters. I believe that by not being able to discuss these issues, it perpetuates the problem and they don't get resolved. I'm so sick of this and it is ridiculous. They know damn well that's way too many tasks for one person and that's a ton of work for somebody. There are other alternatives and solutions. It seems that every time something doesn't work out for that person who presents these preposterous requests or preconditions, they instantly become uninterested in collaborating to find a solution. That's what's most sickening about it. It's as if they take the highfalutin approach of "it's my way or the highway".

Don't get "sneak rolled" by anyone in this industry. The tasks that we do are hard work and we should be properly compensated for them. If they have never done the work themselves, at length, for a period of days and hours, *do not* let them undermine it. We should not be overworked, inundated and manipulated by people who lack knowledge of the amount of work involved in doing one job. If you sense any type of "sneak rolling", tell them to "Do a barrel roll." Watch and see how well they can or can't do that. Then, get the "fox" out of there!

CHAPTER 14

Turning Off the Game

There came a time when I got so frustrated that I decided to turn the game off. I replayed the same level, same area, same boss, and combat fight many times. I tried different strategies until I got frustrated. Rather than rage quitting, I remembered something my great-grandmother and grandmother told me, "Turn the game off."

I got tired of emailing and received no reply. I got tired of applying for in-studio positions to be told they are going to pass on me only to see the same position reposted a month or two later (note: this may be a California job census quota they are doing). I got tired of being told to apply only to be rejected several months later when I needed the job the week I saw the post. I got tired of being told, "We want you to score this game" and then sharing that they are not able to pay me. I got tired of being told, "We want you to be on this AAA game" because of your expertise only for them to not contact me the week they claimed they wanted me to start on the project. I got tired of getting hired on a game, getting the direction of the track, starting to write a music track, finishing it only to be told it is not what they are looking for and receive little to no feedback or direction for it to fit. I got tired of being questioned by developers when I raised my price when I constantly provided quality and professional work and service and when pioneer composers were being paid $1000 for 30 seconds of music in 1993. I got tired of being told I would be referred to other potential clients and they did not follow through. I got tired of being ignored. I got tired of being devalued. I got tired of being forgotten when I

DOI: 10.1201/9781003422815-14

FIGURE 14.1 Turning the Game Off

showed up every single time. I was tired of being consistently professional when most others consistently were not.

I am very cognizant that I am not the only one who has gone through these things as I know a few AAA composers have experienced some of these circumstances.

One of my favourite video game composers, Tim Follin, said he quit games because it was too unstable. Another AAA video game composer mentioned that he did not have work for two years even though he pitched, demoed and wrote emails. However, these are the games people are playing with my life. So, I had to learn to turn the game off.

It came to the point where I applied for a job to vacuum airplanes and was very content with it because I needed a break from the mental games people were playing around with. Whether it is intentional, unintentional, they were aware or not. I turned the game off.

The reset button is real. It is not on consoles for no reason. Our brains need to reset too. We need to disconnect from the mental treadmill we sometimes put ourselves on or other people try to set us up for. Going on long walks and/or hikes, doing chores and running errands. Sometimes, consuming no art at all and separating myself from a computer and all media was the best reset I could give myself. Sleeping was even helpful even when I was not getting the best rest. This is self-care. I did not return until I was ready. It is kind of like when I work out and if my body is sore, then I do not push it. Powering off or resetting is essential because this industry is ruthless just like some of the challenging levels and boss areas/ fights we try to play through. You have to pace yourself. If you choose not to turn the game back on and not play anymore, that is okay too. No one can take better care of you than you. You have to take care of yourself and when and if you decide to return to the game and retry, then you have to be prepared to play as many RPGs at the same time.

CHAPTER 15

Be Prepared to Play as Many RPGs at the Same Time

This ideology might also be attributed to the phrase, "play the long game". However, it's not the same. When I hear "play the long game", it's certainly easier said than done. I hope you are ready to play every RPG that exists and if not, get very familiar because that's exactly going to be the feeling when you are in this industry. So, think and choose the five of the hardest RPGs; two classics, two obscure classics, one very unknown or rare and a new release. These will not be MMOs. They will only be single-player RPGs. The task is to play all of them and try to beat them. Just to clarify, when I say, "beat the game", I mean that there is some kind of ending and the credits roll. The reason I am mentioning this is because there are 100s and 100s of hours that will have to be played in order to possibly beat it. What I am willing to bet is that you will probably finish two out of the five. If you finish one out of the five hardest RPGs, then you have done pretty well to finish two.

When people decide why they want to get into this industry, most people get into it because they have seen one of two reasons.

1. They see someone that looks like (them) that is doing it.
2. It is something that they think they can do, or they would like to do.

DOI: 10.1201/9781003422815-15

It can also be a combination of both and this hooks them. What they find out is that you have to build character. They are going in as they are and regardless, they still have to *build* a character. When you build the character, they have to have certain armour, certain resources, and specific tools, weapons and more, to prepare to play this RPG. This industry is the RPG we are playing.

Now, think of starting in the industry. Then, think of being in the industry for one year, two years, three years, four years, etc. If you are starting your career in community college, like I did, then you are ahead of the game. However, keep in mind that it is considered the second hardest difficulty level to manage. If you are entering the field coming out of college or coming from the film industry and you have no clue what to do, then I am not saying it's unattainable but the equivalent to that is that you are practically playing all five RPGs at the same time every day.

Now, the reason I suggest you finish the one RPG is that what you will learn by playing is how to manoeuvre, how to talk to NPCs and how to level up, all the level grinding that has to be done. The parallel to level grinding in the field is all the proper networking, all the projects that have to get done, all the payments that have to be chased up, and logged (if you are a freelancer), all the business acumen that has to be acquired, the plethora of rejections you will receive, the many emails that will not be answered, and a myriad of other circumstances that will typically betide. This is what I went through in this field to get by. So, if you are not equipped and familiar, the first RPG will never be beaten, which means the *long game* doesn't ever get finished, does it?

The only way to prepare, and in my circumstances, what I trained for was, I played and beat some of the hardest RPG classics. As a child, I did look for all 13 "Shinra Dolls" in *Final Fantasy VII* on PS1 just to try to obtain the Sephiroth Summon and I found one. The average "Shrina Doll" that people found were two if they were lucky. This was in the era when IGN walk-throughs or YouTube gameplays did not exist. You just had to play the game.

With the info I amassed from *Final Fantasy VII*, you gain a feeling for how these types of games play and flow. So, I applied it to *Pokémon Red, Blue, Gold* and *Silver*. Most people have played *Pokémon*, so if you have played it, you have a leg-up. If you beat *Final Fantasy VII*, you have two of the five for experience covered. However, now there are obscure classics to play like *Nier Gestalt, Drakengard, Rogue Galaxy, Project Sylpheed* and more.

There are many different RPGs. *Dark Souls*, Tales of Symphonia, *Final Fantasy X* and *Saga Frontier II*, all the RPGs have different storylines, mechanics, NPCs and areas that you explore. You thought you had to go to the city because everyone told you to go because this is the city that flourishes, but you find out that the city is not what it is cracked up to be. Does this sound a little familiar? Some people have said you *need* to be in Los Angeles, Seattle or New York to have a better chance to work in games. However, you have to go in one direction or another because things are not working out where you are. All the role-playing mechanics have different characters, NPCs, resources and tools that you need to get through, but you have to finish a game. In addition, one may infer that it could be necessary to finish one RPG in order to learn how to play the other RPGs.

Sometimes you do not get good at *Dark Souls*. You can get better and possibly understand the game mechanics because you played games from the 90s like Secret of Mana, Phantasy Star and Chrono Trigger and because these games were not kind to you due to the set difficulty of programming and level design. So, you became proficient and played these types of games, and if you did not learn how to beat a level, then you skipped it. If you did skip, you got thrown into the ocean very quickly and learned to shred water, swim or you would drown. So, hopefully you finished *Dark Souls* and now think you want to play *Xenoblade Chronicles*. These two games do not play the same. So, in your career, you have to adapt. An example would be how someone talks to another person. If you're in a dialogue with someone and they respond negatively, you discover that you cannot talk to that person that way. Other realisation examples that may come to mind are you may not be able to create the same way another creator does. You may not be able to fight these life battles the same way. You may be unable to get through those obstacles the way you once did before, so you have to adapt.

The other major point is that you have to like the game because if you don't like the game that's the key lesson that will be learned. You may not like the game. You may not like to play hard or obscure RPGs. You may not want to finish the game. So, how can you prepare to play a long game, let alone be prepared to play five of the hardest RPGs, if you don't like them because what may most likely happen is you will not finish it. This means that you will quit. This is the harsh truth. In addition, there are many different parts of the game too and not every RPG plays the same.

The only constant that is among them all is the character level grind. The story, characters, NPCs, and mechanics are not equal.

These are crucial things to consider that you may encounter when you work in this field. For example, when you talk to someone and ask them a question, they may not give you all the information but if you ask the same question again and use different words or tone you may get more or less information. This is similar to talking to an NPC with a dialogue tree. You could get introduced to someone else which furthers your main or sidequest odyssey goals. Of course, we know if these sidequests get out, they move us away from the main quest which could be a focal point in the career.

There are sidequests and main quests which go on to whatever your ultimate goals are to what you want to be in the industry. These goals may or may not change but you need to reach something in the end. There are a lot of NPCs and depending on the NPCs you talk to, you may or may not get certain information. There are dialogue trees that may not have been uncovered because you did not know you had to speak to that person twice, or you used a certain verbiage or language to get through the sidequest or main quest. The sidequest directed you to a certain path because you might have been told or thought you needed loot or to obtain tools to get further in your career. So, in order to get to the next step, you thought you needed a specific job, which is the sidequest to hopefully progress further in the main quest. You may have regarded that specific equipment, to go to school or talk to certain people to get scholarships or grants that were needed as well.

What I also learned from this ideology is that I built endurance through mental strength training. As I mentioned before, it started when I was overweight, and I was 220 lbs and I could not fit my clothes anymore and refused to buy any new clothes. So, during the pandemic, I lost about 15–20 lbs in a month by only doing HIIT training and light weights, no gym and I continued the regime the rest of the year. I only had 20 days of recovery which means I worked out the other days in the year. I have maintained my physique ever since because what I was also in training for was wanting to be able to run a marathon. I wanted to start at 2k, 3k and then 5k and finally 10k. I knew I had to get my body and mind in shape and in sync to build and maintain endurance. This is the long game. This served as a two-part goal. My mentality was if I could sustain the training I was doing to run and prepare for the marathon, I would be able to do the marathon in the game industry as well. Not only am I training with video games and metaphorically applying it to the game industry but I am also physically and mentally training to build stamina on an everyday level to continue in the field overall. This is twofold mental conditioning.

Armour – You have to build a mental fortitude like no other to sustain in this field. This is your armour. The highest level of armour is necessary. Tough skin is not enough. If you are not careful, this field space will tear you down and eat you alive, so it's imperative to enter with a good amount of strength, power and mana. This is needed to know how the game is played from the initial competition to many rejections, the wins or "GGs". After so many years, the armour will wear down and you will have to repair it. One way to repair is by "pressing pause" on actions you have steadily been going aggressively at for a long period of time. Take time to assess, reflect and discern how to refine your mental fortitude. During this process, the proper reflection can count as upgrades to your armour should you wish to continue.

Weapons – There are many weapons to choose from to protect and progress. I believe and have chosen my best weapon to be applied, knowledge. The old adage is "knowledge is power". However, I believe the true phrase is "applied knowledge is power". I always share the story multiple times in many interviews via podcasts or articles of how I got into the games industry. The long and short of the story is, I bought a book called *The Complete Guide to Game Audio* Second Edition by Aaron Marks, I read half of the book, I posted my work in a game developer forum, submitted a demo and landed my first paid shipped game called *Electron Flux* (mobile).

So, let's quickly break that down. I gained knowledge from the book and got to a chapter in the book where I immediately applied the knowledge. This resulted in shipping a game that I was paid for without having any mentors, apprenticeships or internships. This is why I believe applied knowledge is the best weapon you can have.

My father told me when I was 9 years old, "Chase, if you would apply yourself as much as you as you play those video games you would be great." At the time, I was having issues in grammar school, and so my

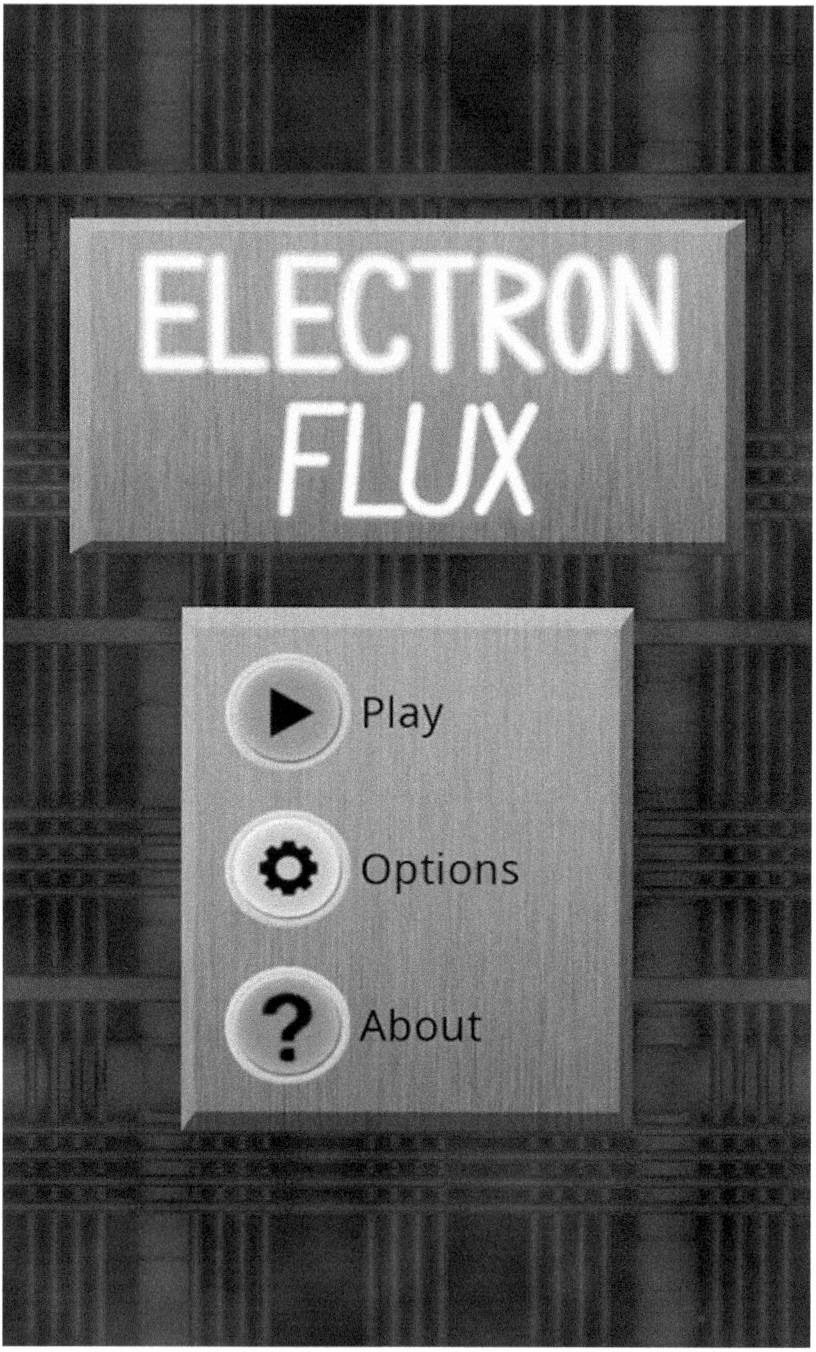

FIGURE 15.1 *Electron Flux* Title Screen

father told me this because he felt I would understand it and apply myself when I was in school. He acknowledged that my interest in video games was substantial. He was absolutely right, and the application compounded over the years, and I exponentially became sharper with the more games I played and beat. For some reason, his words have clicked with me, and I have not let go of the ideology since. This has worked for me in many ways in my career.

Those who say play the long game, it might be easy for them to say, and they may have figured it out because they are in a good financial position and/or the career is good too. However, I would advise listening to the people who don't talk the same and see what they say differently. I'm listening to both with astute ears and then I begin the research afterwards.

If you are fortunate to finish three RPGs at the same time, you will have a higher skill to navigate the field with more assurance. It might be sisyphean to some to complete one RPG but by trying you gain an understanding of the level of difficulty and time it takes to sustain interest and endurance.

I want to make it absolutely clear that I am not saying to play as many RPGs at the same time. I will reiterate. *Be prepared* to play as many RPGs at the same time because for some people's path, depending on their goals and aspirations, this may be the circumstances that they encounter.

CHAPTER 16

True Networking or the Real Truth about Networking

Reach out and say, "Hello."

Since cell phones landed in the consumers' hands and even more so in the social media era, we have technology that *should* make it easier to communicate with one another. We no longer have to write letters and wait (although receiving one of those nowadays is a treat and a joy). But if we are "too busy", lazy and insouciant to send a direct/private message or text to say "Hi, I thought of you today," then there is a serious problem.

Reaching out because you need something versus just reaching out to say "Hi". We are so caught up in our own lives that we barely have time to text. Let alone call one another when in reality you are probably absorbing social media (but NOT socialising), playing video games or binge-watching Netflix. Guess what!? You probably can have a text conversation and do one if not two of those other activities too. A lot of people are confused about networking when they should be working on themselves to strengthen how they would want to be treated. Here is why. An aspect of networking means communicating and that communication needs a recipient. It is not one-sided. If you are always the one reaching out, that is not a good communication line and chances are the "networking" link is dead. Friendships cut both ways. "The doorknob opens to both sides"

DOI: 10.1201/9781003422815-16

and "a cell phone sends as well as receives". You can try to hold on to the network, but the network does not work if it is not nurtured.

Assuming people are busy is another cop out. Sometimes people need to hear from you, but again, it cannot always be them reaching out. If you look at your last call or text from that person and it has been them initiating, then that is a "flag on the play" on your character. This is a problem, and we need to stop giving "extra save files" or passes to people who do it. In my opinion, it is unacceptable. Relationships take effort. If people are upfront and say, "I want to be connected with you. However, I do not have the capacity to keep up, but I will keep you in mind and do my best to reach out when I can" (and THEY DO IT), then that is a decent person to keep part of your network. But I'll share with you a nugget. Those who reach out to you first and are consistent are most likely the ones in your corner. They are genuine. You do not sense "the ask" that is coming. I know very few people that I can count on one hand who have done this with me as I have with them over the years. These folks are there! It is effortless and truthful and that is what genuine communication is. This is one of the pillars that builds a strong network.

16.1 UNDERSTANDING WHAT NETWORKING IS

My definition of networking is making quality friends. Okay, but how do you make quality friendships? What I have come to understand is that everyone's mentality of friendships is different and there are levels to it. I will share with you what I deem to be good friendships: Respect, Consistency and Reciprocation. If you meet someone in the industry and you want to be friends with them, it should not be because of what they can do for you. It should be with some opinion that you think they are fun, cool and exciting. You genuinely like them and they happen to have a cool title or field they work in that interests you. So, if you reach out to your new friend and want to talk or hang out and you are always the one reaching out, there is no reciprocity there. The reciprocity and consistency are on your side but not theirs. So, at that point, you should decide where that friendship lies. Do you cut ties completely or just have that friend as someone you talk to intermittently?

The other key here is not to take it personally. You do not know what is going on in their life, and if they are a new friend, they may not open up to you like that right away. On the other hand, if this friend is cool and reciprocates but is someone who asks a lot of you, you need to determine what limitations of friendship you have with this friend too.

These are just a few things I do not hear being spoken about the deeper steps of friends in your network which is the over arc of networking.

You have to acknowledge that you enjoy at some level the other person's company and/or conversation. This is not transactional. If the energy between you two has tension, then imagine how it will be when you have to work together on a project. How both of you communicate with each other will determine if the collaboration is copacetic or not, especially when there are milestones and deadlines. Just because that game looks amazing and could possibly become popular does not always mean it is worth putting each other through angst and hardship. The game did not make itself appealing, the people behind it did. Therefore, early on, try to determine two things.

1. Does this person treat and speak to me how I would like to be treated?
2. Am I treating or speaking to them how they would like to be treated?

From there, both parties should be able to discern if this is a proper friendship or not. This may take a couple of interactions to reach the conclusion. In the long run, the benefits will be positive. You will either gain a friend that you could end up working with or you could save each other time and energy and create space for the proper person to fill the place of the former.

At the beginning of my career, I wanted to become an assistant of an AAA video game composer. A colleague from LensCrafters had shared that there was a composer signing happening. I recall hearing that the composer of *God of War* (PS2/PSP), Jim Dooley, (*Infamous*) and Cris Velasco were there. Cris ended up not attending. I was under the impression that Cris was the main composer for *God of War* and by not doing my homework properly I discovered it was someone else. Thankfully, I did not make an ass of myself, and I was still respected and asked educated questions. I inquired if any of them needed a composer assistant. The composer of *God of War* replied that he did. I did my due diligence and sent several follow-up emails. I sent these emails for a year until one day, he responded. I still remember the excitement of the response.

Your official Composer's Assistant Chase Bethea

Chase Bethea

Hey Gerard,

This is Chase Bethea. First, I want to say CONGRATULATIONS on winning best video game score for Spiderman: Edge of time. That's a pretty great game and I enjoyed the music!
Also, I found out you have an old school buddy working at CSUN by the name of Scott Glasgow and that you spoke in his Media Composition Classes. That was great!

I have been trying to contact you a couple of times since we met at Dark Delacacies for the composer signing last June 2011. I know you are busy, but as I told you before
I am sure I could be of some help to you. The experience I posses indicates my high qualifications to be your assistant and I would be most happy to apply those skills into working for you. I have a degree in Audio Engineering and I am finishing up my second degree in Music Theory and Composition.

Again, I would love to assist you or possibly even shadow you while you work. I am really excited to work in this industry and I feel like I could learn a lot from you, especially since we already made a connection. My portfolio can be viewed on this website. Please contact me immediately if you are interested in my proposal. My number is 818-217-7921. Call me, Text me, email me whatever. Hope to hear from you very soon.

Best Regards,
Chase Bethea

FIGURE 16.1 Email Correspondence

I was invited over to his house. There, we would discuss expectations, and he even mentions in the email, "getting to know each other better."

I showed up with donuts (because I was raised to not show up without anything when you are invited for the first time) and unbeknownst to me, he was on a strict diet. As I walked into the kitchen, I saw grass on the counter (the kind you see in Jamba Juice) implying this was the healthy focus he was on. I was quite embarrassed, but he assured me the donuts would not go to waste, they would go to his children. (Whew!)

As the day went on, I learned so much. The studio was incredible. He shared his tips and tricks, development stories and workflows for *The Amazing Spider-Man*. I even have the exclusive CD no one has. He also shared how long it took to mix the soundtrack and how he got the job with the development company.

Unfortunately, my work schedule at LensCrafters clashed when he needed me to work. My boss was already on my tail about scheduling, and I would either have to quit and become the assistant for a month or work two days or get another job after or do both. The composer spared me, and I did not do both, but I was pretty depressed that day.

I remember it clearly. I went home and I watched the full season one of Heroes in a day. I talked to my girlfriend at the time and at that moment I knew it was not going to work out with us. Something told me, this is the life of a video game composer, and major sacrifices are going to have to be made, like quitting a job, not eating full meals and stepping away from relationships if I want to become one of the greats.

What came from that was not being his assistant but a friend. Many months later, one day on Facebook, he made a post asking if anyone could help him move. This was the best thing I could have done. That day, I met my future mentors, Ken Jacobsen and Kyle Johnson. In addition, I built trust and reliability. I showed up and in a way that meant something big for him in his life at the time. My actions were genuine. Yes, I would have loved to be his assistant, but the friendship and meeting Kyle and Ken was the better deal. I have known the four of them for over a decade. They all believe in my work, respect me as a person and one of the most talented composers in the industry. It is a huge honour.

Some years later, one day, the composer and I were having drinks at his favourite karaoke spot. He told me, “Chase, you’re a really good guy and great things are going to happen to you.” It brought me to tears (that I held back in front of him). To know how our “ship” started from Dark Delicacies, a comic book store in Los Angeles, to hanging out as friends having a good time and for him to say that to me, it solidified that I made the better decision of not being the assistant. It showed me there is always another path. Thank you, Gerard.

Kyle Johnson is one of the most generous people you will meet in games. He is also a genius. His work on *Burnout, Guitar Hero, Call of Duty* and more is masterful.

I recall going to his house for the first Game Audio Hour meetup. He was completely hospitable. When he saw me again, he said, “I see the work you’re doing, and it is really great.” He proceeded to give me a grand tour of his house and studio. He did not have to say that. Here is a very successful and AAA composer/sound designer/audio director/programmer extraordinaire but I could tell he genuinely believed in my work and me.

Over the years, he imparted so much knowledge when he invited me to his house and was magnanimous in subcontracting me on a couple of gigs. He also started the Game Audio Hour podcast and later on brought me on as a panellist. Kyle was so generous in mastering some of my video game soundtracks and helping me fast track to upgrade my studio as well looking out for me when I was in hard times. To this day, Kyle continues to champion my work and even though I am grateful for the support, I am most thankful for the many years of our friendship.

After helping Gerard, I saw Ken again at what I call the last “Game Audio Network Guild BBQ” in Los Angeles (I literally do not know another that existed after 2014 or 2015). I recall sitting at one of the long patio tables at Inon Zur’s house and having a casual conversation with peers and other AAA composers. Ken then asked me two questions. 1. “Have you worked in Cubase before?” 2. “Have you been a composer’s assistant before?” Both answers were “Yes.” The next thing that surprised me was him saying, “Okay, give me a call next week.” What just happened? What did I do? It turned out that Ken wanted to take me under his wing and be his next intern/assistant.

I learned invaluable information that I will mention parts of later. A short list would include expression maps, deeper knowledge on Steinberg Cubase/Nuendo, complex studio set-ups, the realism of the industry, customer relation management (CRM) and more. Ken helped me with my mixes and even mastered a couple of my video game soundtracks. He is brilliant, kind and a master composer/musician.

I have not told this story to many people but here it goes. Some years ago, I was working at Sam Ash. A colleague and I were conversing, and a man came around the corner and said out loud, "Do you mind if I get some help, please?" I looked at my colleague to see if he was talking to him or me. Then, I asked the man, and he pointed at me.

As I proceeded to help and advise the man to find some monitors for his son, the man asked if I knew how to mix and if so, how much I charge for mixing. I told him the price, and the man said that it was fair.

As I tendered the studio monitors, the customer typically had to have an account within the Sam Ash system. I could not deny that the last name which appeared was startling. I asked the man if he was related to a jazz legend and he said, "I wish." I smiled. He smiled and laughed, and I bid him a good day with my contact information as he requested to inquire about future collaboration for mixing gigs. Much curiosity descended me, so as soon as I was on my break, I researched who he was. Lo and behold, he was related to a jazz legend. I recall the feeling of a random moment that occurred and being close to greatness. Nonetheless, I kept it cool. However, the thought of meeting him never left my mind.

Two weeks later and on a specific work shift, I wondered if the man would return and on the same day that I had that thought, the man did return to the store. He needed some more studio gear for his son. I assisted him with that, and the man exclaimed he was ready to get the mixing process started. He reached out the following week and I began working with him.

The first time we collaborated, he complimented me numerous times on the work I did on his tracks. He listened to it countless times. I remained humbled and thanked him for the opportunity. Over the course of many months, working closely with him was a life-changing experience to behold. I loved his work because it reminded me of mine. His sound is eclectic, unorthodox, energetic and tantalising.

We discovered we were close in creative souls, and through the musical bond, a friendship formed. I had earned his trust, but he had also earned mine. I never asked him to listen to my work until one day he did. When he heard it, he was very impressed. He said to me, "The way you write is incredible. You are already at the level. The world has not listened yet, but they will." It is an honour to say I helped mix one of the jazz legend son's albums.

16.2 CAREER RELATIONSHIPS VERSUS PERSONAL RELATIONSHIPS

Some people have on-and-off relationships and some people have long-term relationships. In relation to a career, freelancers or employees of a company then on and off could occur and/or tenure for employees/returning clients in freelance work. There are four main points that crossover seamlessly between each "ship" (career relationships and personal relationships). They are personality, actions, willpower and accusations.

Personality is your character, habits and thoughts, and every person is unique with these traits. These qualities create attractions for the other person. Some have charisma and that lands them a job or gig just as much as it lands them a new date.

Actions determine if your ship will endure or end short. Some actions become habits that can result in promotions, contract terminations, new editions to the family or tension between siblings.

Willpower is the most important thing. It covers areas like trust, patience and special vibes that will guide you through these "ships." Willpower determines how strong you are inside.

With personality and willpower combined, it will either do things that are good or bad in a "ship." A couple of examples that could be considered bad things are cheating and withholding some imperative information from your significant other or business partner. A couple of examples that could be considered good things are listening and showing undivided attention when needed (career or personal). Showing up when committed and you gave your word you would.

Accusations can and will kill any ship. If all the facts are not there, there is no reason to blame, shame or pass any judgement. It's the "insta-penultimate-kill". Once this occurs, trust will instantly dissipate and will almost be impossible to rebuild. If an employer, client, significant other or family member, did this it would be your right to leave and not ever return. Some people do not appreciate a good person until they are gone, and usually by the time they do, it is too late. They always regret it.

I discovered in my ninth year in my career that a lot of these exchanges are closely related to personal relationships and there are some parallels.

When you are interested in someone or they are interested in you typically, the next step is for you both to go on a date. Why and how did it happen? Why would they go on a date with me? To some degree, they trust you. Think about development teams or companies. Why would they hire you? To some extent, they trust you.

The takeaway from these anecdotes and examples is that there was trust. Trust in being a man of my word. Trust that I would show up every time and trust that I would deliver. People have to trust you at some level and to some capacity. The very experienced ones can read your energy quickly and sense this. This is sometimes an innate human trait that is amplified through life experiences. Trust comes first. It cannot be faked. It is not the mindset of only making friends. It is the reliance of integrity towards someone that you choose to interact with. Friendship comes after and that takes time, and over the duration, more trust is built which presents opportunity.

CHAPTER 17

Hey! Listen!

"Words will take you far, but actions will take you a lot farther." I came up with this quote due to my experience in the industry regarding how most people talk a good game. They really do. Unfortunately, a lot of people do not take action after the words. It sounds good out loud, but they get in their own way. Sometimes our own fear about this holds us back tremendously. It's about the quality of work. The pandemic was tough for a lot of people. We took the opportunity to do charity, build up knowledge and share with one another. However, learning when to say "No" had never felt so strong.

Checkpoint 1: So, I was happy to receive a message from this group of video game music organisers. They wanted to know if I was interested in being a panellist or putting something together for their event. When they reached out in the initial email, they allegedly "didn't have any money" but they said they could offer me some promotion.

Alright, so there are a lot of issues with this already. I am an established composer, and I have volunteered a lot of my time especially in 2020 and the years before. I'm glad that they like my music and that they heard it, but to only offer promotion alone was not going to be enough. So, I wanted to negotiate a little.

I wrote back and inquired what kind of panel they were trying to do because they never said in the initial ask. I informed them that typically, at the time, I get paid $250–$500 to guest speak/be a panellist. In addition,

DOI: 10.1201/9781003422815-17

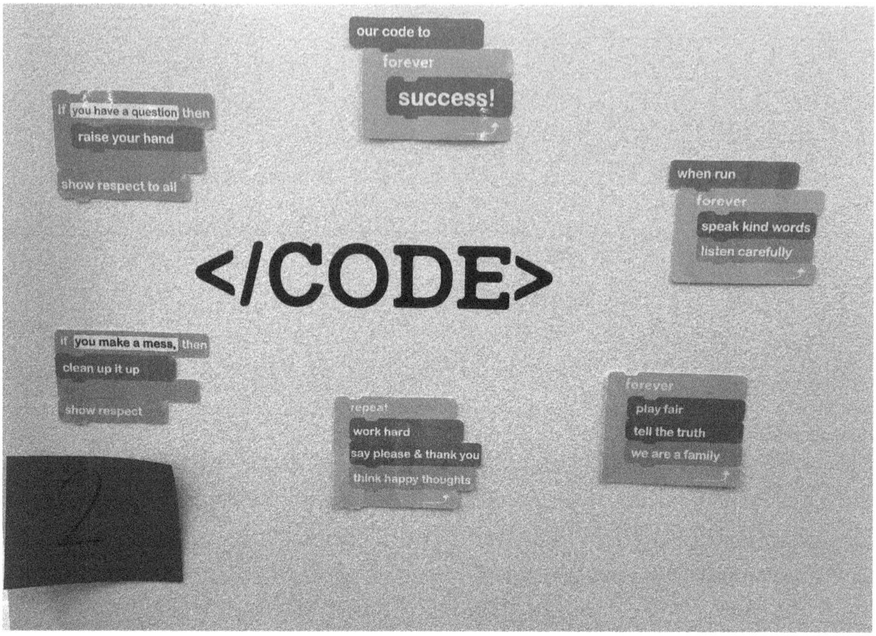

FIGURE 17.1 Code

before I agree to participate, I would need to know a couple of things, if they were open to the discussion.

The first counteroffer was that I could write the theme music of the event or have my music played during the intermission. I would be asked to come back to be a panellist or performer if they were to have future events. I believe since they were not offering any compensation that there was no risk to them as I was presenting the music that I have. I did not ask them to pay for the theme. What became apparent was that these people were really inexperienced and it was really annoying.

They declined my counteroffer. They thanked me for the thoughtful response, but they couldn't offer what I was asking for. I found this to be somewhat manipulative. They were going to try to get something out of me but not offer anything in return except for promotion, which is something most of us can create and do ourselves. Yet it's only to promote their event, not any of my future works on its own.

The rest of the email relayed that they could not offer me what I'm looking for and they didn't know how big the event was going to get and that they were trying to organise something to help people with the isolation during the pandemic. In addition, they didn't want to waste my time, wished me well with my future endeavours and pretty much signed me off.

I had a lot of "ducking" issues with this email. 1. They did not do their thorough homework on putting this event together. 2. The game music community is huge and they're going to support anything that anyone does involving games + music. Look at MAGFest which I am almost positive these organisers have attended. The majority consensus is that when you organise a video game music community, it blows up in popularity. So, this sent a slight "Toledo Bull" signal to me that the organisers did not do the research, or they were lying to me, in which I felt my intelligence being insulted. 3. A lot of us have done a ton of charity work, especially established composers such as myself. Why should I continue to do charity work when I barely get paid by some of the developers themselves who don't want to pay for music because it's so cheap to get it from other composers who devalue the work? So, I was in shock that they didn't even consider having a discussion. They straight up wrote me off.

In their reply, they still did not tell me what the panel was going to be about and did not tell me who was going to be on the panel. It was very disappointing, and I was pissed off about it.

I truly wish negotiations would be a mental practice people do before requesting favours. I believe the email should have said this,

> We think the counteroffers are fair. At this time, we can't offer anything right now. We understand that promotion is not a consolation. Yet, we were hoping that you will be interested in participating. If you still would like to partake, this is the time of the panel and these are the ideas we're thinking about. Let us know your thoughts.

Have your "ducking" information in order before you reach out to people. Know the climate. Know the history. Other music + game organisations have figured out how to pay their guests, panellists and performers. So, why is it a mystery to not follow the same standard that has been established for 20 years?

There is another untruthful colloquial phrase that people say too much and that is, "We don't have money." I think this sentence needs to stop being said. People have money or they would truly be on the street and the majority of people who say this are not homeless. How about saying, "We do not have the budget for that right now," or what I think is more truthful, "We do not want to pay for that." Although trying to put something up rather than nothing would be nice, saying "We don't have money" comes off as deceptive. In addition, those that say the phrase show up to all the conferences that are not cheap to attend, travel wise and/or rent booths or tables to demo their games or merchandise. Most likely, it was not free to go, so where did the money come from? I'm really sick of this. This behaviour is what perpetuates unkind practices that prevent the industry from maturing and thriving and wears harshly on the mental health of creatives.

Checkpoint 2: One year, I was in a virtual meeting breakout room with five people and an industry colleague/friend of mine. I was previously in a different breakout room with someone else, who I will refer to from now on as "A", who practiced sound design and music. However, upon entering the breakout room, since we did not do introductions, they didn't know that I was a video game composer.

My industry colleague, whom I met at E3 three years ago, was also in the breakout room. We have been following each other's work since. So, the colleague had said specifically to me, "Hey Chase, so, if I get this development grant for this game I am producing would you want to score the music?" and I replied, "Yes."

Now, there was another guy in there who worked at Magic Leap and said, "Wow, do you see how that happens 'A'?" and "A" replies, "Yeah." He continues, "I do music and sound too and if you want to check out *both* of our works, you know, that would be great."

Okay, I'm not averse to working with somebody but here is how that approach came off. "A" does not have a rapport with my friend, I do. If you were in a group of people and there were three girls and two guys. You and one girl have been talking, and she says, in front of the group, "Hey, would you like to go to this concert with me? Maybe we can get dinner beforehand." Let's say we do not know qualifications except that you have some rapport, and if you are available and interested in the concert, then you agree to go. So, then the other guy jumps in and says, "What about me? I wanna go with you too. Why don't you ask both of us and see who is available/interested?" How would it make you feel? It looks awkward and probably could be seen as being a hater and possibly desperate.

It's rude to do that, so don't do it. It's just that simple. Yes, it's about who you know, however, the point is respecting the fact that the rapport has been built to get to know that person. I obviously have that rapport. I don't believe the approach is to chime in and say, "Hello, I do this as well. I think I'm just as qualified." Do you know each other? Do you have a rapport? Did you ask? This is not good practice and it's not good manners.

Everyone in this industry is a human being and likes appreciation. Let us not forget and do better.

Checkpoint 3: Due to a highly unfortunate event, there was a catalyst that occurred. Many people rallied and claimed that they were interested in diversity, equity and inclusion once the George Floyd incident happened. However, that situation should not have been the impetus for DEI to be acknowledged and represented. Sadly, I was perspicacious, and I thought it was ruse and temporary. I turned out to be correct because in 2021 there were signs of it dying out. Some companies have had people in a position to represent the opportunity for DEI, but other companies shut down those departments within four years. It comes down to putting your money where your mouth is. If you say you're going to do something, do it all the way. Don't do it for a short period of time because someone lost their life. Keep integrity and stay honest. If you don't want to participate, then don't, but if you do, then stay consistent.

Checkpoint 4: In Spring of 2022, I found myself rewatching seasons 1–5 of "Better Call Saul", a phenomenal show that has so much depth beyond its story. It's incredible. I had already watched season five when it was released but something happened that was subtle, and I became penchant to rewatch them. One day, I was scrolling YouTube and the character that plays "Hector Salamanca" (Mark Margolis), a thumbnail appeared. Without a second thought, I clicked the video and to my surprise, the character "Mike Erhmantraut" (Jonathan Banks) was sitting across from Mark. It turned out to be a general conversation about lessons they learned in their career, their beliefs of the industry as well as some anecdotes. It was completely wholesome, and I thoroughly enjoyed watching them talk casually. Purely magical.

One anecdote that came up was about commercials. Mark shared that he did a commercial for Volvo and the sales irony that it had. Jonathan replied, "I'd do a commercial if they asked me . . . nobody ever asked me." That shit hit me so hard. Here is an actor who has been nominated for Emmys, been on "Sanford and Son", working in the industry for 30 plus years and he never got asked to do a commercial! It stuck with me. It was something that was on my mind for a couple of days. Then, I realised why.

There are some people in this industry who claim they want to help you but never follow through with their actions. They will host your work on their site to get them more work, but when they have big opportunities, you don't get that call. So, when a new big game releases and you see others that you know or have spoken to within the industry, whose work is not on that specific company's website, post about being part of a project, my mind used to wander. I could not help but think of what Jonathan Banks said and relate it to my career. Here is what it sounded like to me in my mind at the time.

"I would have liked to have been part of that AAA game if they asked me . . . but no one ever asked me."

The advice that typically goes around is to let people know what you do. Tell people you are looking for work and the type of work you want. When you say the type of work you want and what you do multiple times in different forms (email follow-ups, social media posts of your work, blogs, YouTube videos, newsletters, etc.) and those people who have hiring power see it, like those posts, engage in it and then don't ask you to be part of the big project but someone else you know is involved, it hurts. For me, it's not seeing the action occur one time that is hurtful. I have tough skin. I am speaking of the steady pattern of occurrences of seeing it betide for some years.

It's not to compare or be the victim. The perspective I'm pointing out is to cut the bullshit. Do not have my work on your website. Do not bother saying you have work for me and never follow-up or when I follow-up with you, monthly or bimonthly, that you do not respond or that gig you mentioned that you wanted me to be part of has "poofed" and disappeared. Please do not bother trying to sell me a bunch of stories that nobody is buying.

Checkpoint 5: Industry Issues with Communication: We need to work on our communication skills. When someone recommends you for a

> volunteer position and takes the time to think of you, you say thank you. When someone recommends you for any type of position if you have another colleague that you know. The person who recommends can definitely answer your questions versus the person you know, even if they are your friend, sure you can ask but that person did not recommend you.

When you apply for a job in a cold email, the polite thing to do would be to answer, even if it takes you a week to respond. It does not take that long to think about what you want to say in a week. In Uni, it was told to us by the director of the program to respond to emails within 24 hours. I think this is a little unrealistic to do all the time. I have come across people who want responses from you within three minutes or within an hour. If you are one of those people who have that super quick time, what I call "communication expectation", you should consider being a little more reasonable. There should be a sensible understanding that people have lives too (i.e. partners, children, many jobs, etc.). I know that people are busy and a week's time to reply is possibly a good enough runaway. Most of us have emails that we receive on our cell phones. I believe they can send emails too. I know and understand that emails can get lost or go to spam. However, my case is speaking about the two or more emails that have been sent. If you think that you are someone who is going to miss it, then start it, leave it unread and mark it as important. Most of these email service platforms created all these tools for these "r&e's" (reasons and excuses) to be non-existent.

A polite way to respond could be, "Hi, we are not looking for any of those services at the moment. Thank you for the email. Please check in with me at a later date." or "Hi, we are not looking for any of those services at the moment. We do not accept unsolicited requests. Our website will show openings of any positions at our companies. Thank you."

Another reply could be, "Hi, thank you for your email. However, we respectfully are not interested in those services. Best wishes."

It's not hard and it does not take long to draft. People make it hard, and I do believe some people intentionally do not reply. However, this has a long-lasting effect on people's minds, and we wonder why we are in the situations and mindsets we are in the field about mental health and trying to make it better. This is a portion of the bad habits because it stems further and further into other issues but could be mitigated with small practices and consistency with good, solid communication. There is a solution.

I have heard from some people that there is a fear of hurting people's feelings if they send those types of rejection replies. However, if the right communication tools are used, then those fears could disappear, and there are right communication tools. I think it's ridiculous at this point that for as long as the industry has been around, this communication etiquette has not been practiced often by the higher-ups such as CEOs at companies all the way to people on small teams. The social skills are fucked! I have not seen this talked about often, but it is something that should be addressed. These are some of the responses that have worked when you receive these types of emails or messages. Yes, it may sting. No one likes being rejected. It will have some type of effect, but I believe that by being ignored, it will have a much longer mental effect. Some people naturally like closure. Some people naturally want to resolve things. I do not think that people want to feel shitty or upset. So, if there is an opportunity to refrain from saying, doing or not saying or doing stupid things because of what you think the response is going to be, then take it. As long as you were not maliciously trying to be detestable, then most likely the person will be okay. So, just reply. Think about what you want to say before you say it and have the conversation. Keep it real. It's really that easy.

When someone seeks advice from someone, they take the time out of their day to meet with them, a follow-up thank you email is a good gesture. It does not take that long to draft. Here is a follow-up message example: "Hey, thanks so much for meeting with me yesterday and sharing your knowledge with me. I really appreciate it." This goes a long way, believe it or not, it really does because it re-solidified that this person truly values the time given. The person making the time to meet with them did not have to make that time they wanted to. In my decade plus of giving so much advice to newcomers who have asked for my time, barely a handful have done this. I find it quite fascinating as most of the outreach emails are paragraphs or more with questions but the simplest two or three sentences are not sent once they get what they want. Professionally, this type of etiquette goes the extra mile and can make a bigger impact. If this was practiced more, I believe the field and community could be stronger and strengthen more positivity.

It was time to speak on this because I saw many immediate solutions coming left and right and I still kept hearing excuses. So, I call bullshit. We can do better, and we should.

CHAPTER 18

Navigating Emotional Intelligence

I believe the key tactic to navigating emotional intelligence is building an environment that understands the interpersonal skills that are needed in order to be successful in the industry. This includes traversing and paving the paths where you may not be acknowledged and accepted in order to stand strong and radiate in your purpose.

I learned quickly at a young age to have interpersonal life skills and to be "good in the room". Although I had a few mentors who showed me how, such as my Mum, Ken Jacobsen, Gerard Marino and Kyle Johnson, I still had to polish these skills daily. I had to learn, practice, remind, repeat and replay. I had to glean from the knowledge passed to me that worked, apply it to my personality and experiment in those meet-and-greet events.

When I was at Game Dev' Drink Up in LA, I used to put this pressure on myself that I had to meet at least five people. I felt that I was trying to connect with people to get work or for people to like me because I was told people want to work with who they like. Most people want to work with their friends. After attending and trying so many times, I discovered that the approach I was taking was not effective. I did not feel like it was making quality connections. So, I changed my goal to just meet one person. This goal adjustment was a lot more attainable. If I ended up having a quality connection that led to work, then that would be icing on the cake.

DOI: 10.1201/9781003422815-18

This relieved a lot of stress and burden from me as it resulted in enjoying future drink-up events from there forward. I was even able to help a friend, who was an introvert, navigate the event easier. By adjusting and lessening my expectations, I assisted in helping my friend have conversations with people they did not know. My support provided comfort and made it painless for them to navigate the social atmosphere.

Emotional cognizance and intelligence are constant stat practice.

My mum taught me how to do this. I recall being at an awards ceremony in an auditorium. My mum was receiving an award that night for Best Actress. She told me, "Look around you, Chase. Do you see anyone that looks like us?" "No," I replied. "You belong here. Get comfortable," she said. Her words were so profound that I never forgot them. So, when I decided to enter the game industry, I recalled what she said, knowing I was the minority. In addition to acknowledging, I would be the prime example of a minority that knew that they belonged and brought high value to the table. However, in this odyssey, I have identified that it is not enough, you need more. "Practice makes perfect so when perfect is practiced then perfection is flawless." This is something I wrote many years ago and through cogitation I recognised something more that was axiomatic.

There is a difference between practicing and being conditioned. You can either decide to practice or not. Even when you are practicing, you are being conditioned to the process of action you are doing. Therefore, you are either conditioning yourself to practice the action or not practice the action.

If you have ever played *FFX* (*Final Fantasy X*), you may recall the Thunder Plains area. If you want to obtain a special ultimate weapon for Lulu, a character in your party, you will have to dodge 200 lightning strikes. Let us pretend these lightning strikes occur in your video game industry career. So, you practice dodging the lightning 200 times and your reward is your mind being conditioned to now be perspicacious about seeing lightning betide and being able to dodge it. The chances of lightning hitting you now, which will slow you down or worse crippling you, will be very slim.

Without the choice of choosing to practice to learn how to dodge, you would not be conditioned to become better at the action. If you choose the action to not learn how to dodge, you could possibly be conditioning yourself to be struck by lightning more often which will cause multiple setbacks. Ultimately, the choice weapon of practice is yours to decide. I believe it is best to balance your stat traits accordingly so that you show up as your best self on a daily basis to provide higher value to yourself and to others.

CHAPTER 19

The Imposter Syndrome Facade

The short of it is if you are burger flipper, auto mechanic, plumber or brain surgeon who claims they compose video game music and or design sound effects for games (i.e. they claim to work on their craft in their spare time, they claim to have participated in game jams, been paid for their or and shipped games) but never have any proof that you did those things. KNOCK IT OFF! Let us define what imposter means.

Imposter: *a person who pretends to be someone else in order to deceive others, especially for fraudulent gain.*

Syndrome: *a group of symptoms which consistently occur together, or a condition characterised by a set of associated symptoms.*

So, unless you are that burger flipper I mentioned that never has proof of what they claimed, then where the fuck did you get that idea that you have "imposter syndrome"? Aren't you doing the damn thing? Didn't you just write game music for that Retro Platform Jam last week? Didn't you just post about the level design work you did for the game studio a couple of hours ago? Weren't you paid by that indie studio for your work on that one game? Did you just answer, "Yes"? Oh, that's what I thought. Nothing about that sounds like a consistent occurrence of deceptive or fraudulent

DOI: 10.1201/9781003422815-19

claims or opinions. So, unless you truly are "posing", please quit that negative mindset shit and keep kicking arse!

I have noticed that the industry has a nasty habit of adapting words or phrases because they catch on but may not apply or be the right thing to apply to. We say "imposter syndrome" because someone heard it before and if it feels applicable to their situation, then it's the "best" way to describe it. That may not be true. We lose more identity through copying. If it's not "imposter syndrome" and it's just hard work that you have a hard fucking time getting through, then it's a hard time you're fucking getting through. "Self-doubt" and "hard times". The industry needs to be more selective with words to describe these problems we face ethically, politically, emotionally and professionally. Come up or use phrases that actually describe the true feeling, not use one that we think describes it because it's a buzzword or phrase.

When we misuse a phrase in a superfluous manner and enough people exploit the phrase, then there will be two definitions of that phrase. "Imposter Syndrome" is a classic example where it's been frivolously used so many times that it improperly describes the actual feeling.

What you're probably feeling is insecurity. The definition of that is *lack of confidence or assurance: self-doubt.* It's okay to not know what you're doing. The point is to do it so that you learn how to know what you're doing. Preparedness triumphs insecurity and transforms into confidence. Your challenge, should you choose to accept it, is to change your mindset. So, if you feel unprepared, self-conscious or unsure, let's individually evaluate ourselves, the feelings and say something like "unsure," but I do not suggest you say, "I am feeling imposter syndrome".

> Words do matter and they matter because they tell us how we feel about ourselves and other people.
>
> – CHRIS DO

So, we need to think before we speak and choose our words wisely.

CHAPTER 20

Low HP

In the fall of 2020, I had been drained for some months. In fact, in January 2021, I told myself. I would not seek talks to do or submit unless it was truly important and worth the time. I would focus on projects that I truly wanted to work on that would grow my career. I felt the burnout before. It happened in August 2020, and it was not good. So, at the beginning of the year, I did not write music for a week, and it felt great!

I went through some emotional maelstroms on August 14, 2021. So much that I decided to not be on social media unless I absolutely needed to be. Meaning, that I *had* to post or promote something important that I had already agreed to prior. Let me say that doing nothing extra, just focusing on one thing was SO nice.

For some weeks, I didn't stream my video game composing process and people started to notice my absence. I had made an impact but what was going on behind the scenes was that I was searching desperately for inspiration in my industry again. Something I haven't truly seen in a few years. I am not talking about new games being released or podcast episodes. I am talking about this majestic feeling that is raw and pure. That electrifying thing that gets you so charged you can be on it for months, if not years.

Although we have adapted and manoeuvred through the pandemic and made astounding accomplishments, in my humble opinion, "we" (as in our industry), do not have that "blue flame". The blue flame is the hottest form of fire that burns and in the context of this analogy, it is the pure, authentic passion that is missing from the field. The truth is that the industry is just a flame that is kindling. This is okay as there will be a new golden age soon.

DOI: 10.1201/9781003422815-20

As a close friend, "Doc," told me, "the period of plateau is just as important as the period of growth." It's very true. Feeling spent beyond measure had me down and led to mild depression. I watched my days waver with progress as I struggled to get through most of my project milestones. Some days, I just wanted to lie in bed. Ironically, and thankfully, opportunities were still happening. I was still being requested to be on panels, give talks and demo/bid for new projects. For once, I wasn't seeking the opportunity, it was coming to me. Something I worked very hard for over a decade.

More importantly, I locked into doing my own thing. If people wanted to reach me, they would text or call. If not, I wouldn't hear from them. If I had enough energy during this period to reach out, then I would but I would not be emotionally disturbed anymore if they didn't. This felt nice. Technically, I'm not doing nothing, I'm just doing less. In both instances, when I took that week off and when I stopped going on social media for weeks, emailing people, hunting down opportunities and just focusing on *one task a day*, doing less helped me tap into my emotions. Things that were ambiguous and that I struggled creatively with on some days, but the following day of that cryptic fog was cleared when it was time to check out.

In my years, I have noticed the industry does not practice doing less enough. It enacts and sometimes celebrates "crunch", then lays off the staff instead of giving positive rewards. I do wonder if the video game field took at least a week off from everything, what paradigm shift would betide? Would people operate with more kindness and care for themselves and each other? Would more introspection occur? Would creativity flow more abundantly within? I think this time off should be practiced. Let's press pause and resume when one is properly refreshed to replenish our HP.

CHAPTER 21

Shield Mode

I attended a concert that spotlighted composers of different ethnic backgrounds. I decided to approach a famous composer whose work I admired from numerous films and concert music. When I introduced myself, he was nice but distant. I wondered at that moment if we had met before and if I am a member of this organisation in which he co-founded, why is he acting this way? I thanked him for creating the organisation and he expressed his gratitude. He proceeded to walk away and take a photo with the fellow composers whose work was being featured that night. "Nice meeting you," he said and walked away. At that moment, I felt as if he didn't care too much about who I was and what I did and that left me feeling awkward. This person started an organisation for people of colour and there seemed to be zero interest in learning about other paying members of the organisation.

Later on that evening, I decided to talk to the conductor during the intermission. I introduced myself and before I got my idea out, the composer I spoke to earlier was standing next to me. I thought to myself, "Do I introduce my idea now?" I decided that I didn't care when to do it and based on my previous experience I just had with that composer, this was my opportunity. I said my peace. After my proposal to the conductor, the composer said, "That's a great idea". Of course, he thought the idea was great, but it was my idea. He proceeded to interject into the conversation I had with the conductor as his piece was the last piece played before the intermission, so he wanted to compliment them. I stood there. I didn't care that I was interrupted (something that was rude to do and would normally

DOI: 10.1201/9781003422815-21

bother me). However, I wanted to wrap up my conversation with the conductor properly. So, I waited patiently until their conversation ended and promptly resumed until intermission ended. The composer finished his conversation and went about his business to speak to someone else.

I say all this to say that egos in Hollywood are ridiculous. You get to a certain status, and you become too busy to respond to fan mail. Too busy to learn about the community that pours their money and time into attending events organised by them to thank them for coming to support your fucking work! It's fucking bullshit! Even in the success that I reached thus far, I respond to as many messages and/or emails as I can within context. Solicited cold calls that come to me. I keep it brief and honest because I believe it's the right thing to do. I have been on the receiving end of being ignored. Many, many times and I understand one has to filter some messages out. However, the ones who are praising your work or looking for internships, if you made something that is supposed to help elevate the culture, you have a responsibility to be more involved and engaged and if you can't be that then say so. Do not just disappear. I believe that responsibility is owed to the community. Sure, I understand that it is not always possible to respond to everything but damn, at least try to those that make the effort who support you. Karma is real. What you put out is what you get back. If it is not a big ask, just invest a little. It is highly likely to possibly help return in good favour two times over. Ignoring people leaves a nasty stain. Don't be "Hollywood", be humble. And as you grow in this field, try your best to shield yourself from those egotistical types. Keep that mode up. Trust me, it's better for your career and your mental stability.

CHAPTER 22

Sidequests

As you read this chapter, these are anecdotes and experiences of my own that I endured. As the reader, take them as you will and try to understand and comprehend the many vantage points.

In this book, I talk about anecdotes that are not always uplifting and positive, but they are real. These are the experiences. These people's thoughts became their words, and their words became their actions. Sometimes, a lot of these words have come from the actions of their character, and this affects how other people's work is altered by those actions and the person's character.

The only thing to do is learn how to navigate better, recover semi-swiftly or take time to recover properly and adjust the game plan. So, you can't control other people's actions, but you can control how you respond. This response in the moment is hard to practice because as humans we instantly run off emotions.

If you are not practiced and cognizant to realise these things in the moment, you will fail and fail a lot. Unfortunately, these circumstances become these anecdotes, and they develop into what they are until they aren't.

What I do wish for is that better choices are made, healthier choices are made, and thinking before speaking is practiced so that the coping thoughts, such as "it's fine" or "it is what it is," are diminished or become non-existent. However, this would be indicative of the person doing the introspection work. Again, you are only in control of yourself, so the best thing you can do is make the healthy and better decisions that you believe are the most positive outcome of it, and if you instinctively think it may cause a problem, try to find the path that is least disrespectful and

DOI: 10.1201/9781003422815-22

resistant. Doing this may bring some perspective to how it will affect the other person. I believe the conflation of some level of empathy and cognizance is the only thing we can at least try or attempt.

22.1 SCENARIOS OF WHICH HOW I THOUGHT SOMETHING MAY TURN OUT

What I thought would happen? “Hi, I do music for games” – Oh let me introduce you to someone who is developing a game [The game industry is small right? We should know someone who is developing a game]. This only happened a few times in the 11 years I attended GDC and 14 years I have worked in the games industry.

What actually happened – Hi, let me introduce you to this composer.

Stop. Think. Is this a composer with work overflow? No? Okay. Well, sure, we can be friends but is that where it stems? This person’s ambition or work ethic may not match mine, but people were very fast to always introduce another composer to a composer who may not be in a position to hire. I understand people’s careers change to become better and grow but that intro to someone who does not ascend is a dead end.

This did not just happen with composers. I heard this happens with graphic design friends too. Where people will try to introduce other graphic designers to graphic designers.

How about thinking carefully before introducing people to someone besides thinking they are cool. Think of this as business too. How do you think they will be able to benefit each other at this moment in time? We are both not guaranteed to be around in five to ten years when one or both of us are at bigger companies that hopefully pay us well and where we can possibly give leg-ups.

Also, not everyone who does the same discipline wants to meet one another. The industry is competitive, and if it wasn’t, then NDAs would probably not exist and everyone would have work and work would be abundant, especially for freelancers. We would have more work than we can handle.

Let us try to ask ourselves this question to both parties you would like to introduce. “Hey, I have this friend, they do x. I think they are cool but also are at this stage in their career. Do you think that you would want to meet them?” If both parties say yes, then introduce them. If something great comes out of it, then that is a plus. If one party says no or they are not interested or both do not agree to meet, then it’s probably best to leave it there.

Do not get me wrong, I do understand that the person who wants to introduce their cool friends wants others to be friends too and it does not come from a place of being ungrateful. I am asking to let us evaluate the thought of personalities and present benefits for all parties before making an impulsive introduction and not base it on a similar skill or discipline.

Of course, this is just my opinion due to *many* experiences where no one asked me if I wanted that introduction or not. When I put into practice what I just suggested earlier, where I asked both parties first if they would like to be introduced, they appreciated and respected it more and those friendships did flourish into helping each other further in their career and endeavours.

In rare cases over several years, I did meet other composers or game audio professionals who did lead to some career growth, and I am most grateful. However, most of those introductions I made on my own. Audio people seem to have a knack for finding one another. We do not need extra magnets. It's either that or the universe loves bunching us together.

What I did see is those introductions that I mentioned before, betide for certain folks in the industry. I watched it over and over. Many times, for many years. I had to find out for myself. It was like playing an open-world game, you're looking for that NPC that is going to give you that item or tell you where to go in order to further your progress in the game, but you're lost and lost for hours. You go back to the NPC and talk to them thinking that you missed something until you realise there is a glitch. The game does not tell you there is a glitch, so you either have to start the game over or figure out how to bypass that to not lose the time, effort, items and more you busted your ass to have. When you do figure out how to make progress in the game either by starting over or bypassing the glitch, there is tremendous exponential growth that occurs because you found your way without the guide or the intro.

22.2 OTHER SIDEQUESTS I HAVE TAKEN INCLUDE THINGS THAT I THOUGHT WOULD RESULT IN MORE WORK BUT DIDN'T

- Going to GDC. There is a myth that occurs that if you go to this conference and that you'll have a lot of opportunities to work but that's not true and has value and the value had to be timed with people's interest.
- Being nominated for an award in the industry. This did nothing for me. Nothing. It was not the career booster that I anticipated it would

be at the time in my career. I did not gain any new clients from this. However, I am still very proud of that nomination to this day because it was only my sixth year in the field and I was among some heavy hitters. Most of which are still in the game.

- Being signed to a publisher. For some reason, this is not appealing either. I seemed to think that being seen along with the "top dogs" would attract top work. I was wrong. I still had to grind. Work hard. Build my name. Every day. Every year.

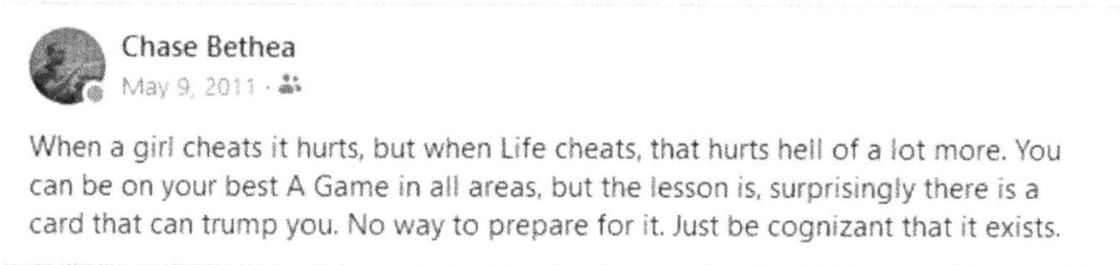

FIGURE 22.1 Facebook Memory

(continued quote) "So that you don't get caught off guard."

What I mean by "life cheating" is when the odds are against you, the unexpected things (i.e. car breaks down, unexpected repairs, random family matters and more) betide all at once. This includes things out of your control. Rejections from scholarships, jobs, pitching for gigs, lay-offs and more occur simultaneously. Reflecting on this, it baffles me that these words were constructed and that I posted them. I am grateful because I knew my future self would need to see and read them again.

In this field, there have been many weeks where I have felt that life has cheated and it still hurts, no matter how much you prepare because when you have passion, you can't destroy that. Passion becomes vulnerable to open spots and unfortunately, it's not possible to protect all sides. However, now, deep down, I believe that even when "life cheats", passion will always win the game.

22.3 "PLEASE HELP"

If anyone has played the game, *Darkstone*, they will know the voice I am speaking of when you're getting "wrecked" by enemies. The voice that yells this describes the voice in my mind as I have had to navigate the field the past decade.

For as long as I can remember, I have looked for help. If you know me personally, meaning I have let you in, you will know I am someone who does not ask for help because my standards for consistency have been let down countless times in the past. When I decided to ask for help, it was turned down. One of my many goals was to be represented by Bob Rice. Bob Rice (rest in peace) is someone who was one of the first "Video Game Composer agents/PR"; he represented people like Inon Zur, Jeff Broadbent and more. After him, came Greg O' Connor Read, Jayson Napolitano and eventually Sarah Kovats of "Kraft/Engel".

Getting the attention of these people has been hard because it depends on the success of the game. The pipeline of attention goes like this.

So, the biggest hang-up is that most game studios do not or do not know how to market the game properly which results in a subpar release in popularity. So, it doesn't get the attention of the people you want help from to push your career.

I tried many times to get this representation. With *Deity Quest*, I reached out to a few popular game audio public relations agencies (that mostly represent AAA composers) and they told me the game was not popular enough and to come back with something else.

FIGURE 22.2 Flow Chart-1

Another popular game audio public relations company wanted to run a public relations campaign for the *Deity Quest* soundtrack for $600, and with the game, *Aground*, he told me that "I'm almost there" in terms of "reaching a level of notoriety", I presumed aka people giving a shit. I don't like to assume, however, I am good at figuring out context clues.

I met and sat with an agent who works at Kraft/Engel at Gamesound Con in 2019, received the "okay" to add her as a friend on Facebook to continue the conversation and never was accepted or received any follow-up correspondence.

I made a list of agencies and managers and called all to be ignored.

I reached out to composers who used to be on a veteran AAA agent's roster. I received an email introduction from one composer to that agent and emailed him only to hear crickets.

I worked with a public relations person in Poland, where things seemed to have a decent working relationship with some PR work but there was a massive language barrier between English and Polish. The relationship had to end due to multiple misunderstandings.

I decided to create my own agent/manager and approached a friend who was brilliant with data analytics but didn't work in the game industry. I felt that with her knowledge, I would be able to coach her into a super manager for the games industry operating behind the scenes. If I combined the knowledge of the industry with her knowledge of business management and navigation, I could have the upper hand for the proper representation I seeked for so long. She was able to draft emails for leads, see charts of companies where the money was going to projects on websites and customise/refine my CRM system. Then, the pandemic hit, and although we did our best to work together, the mental toll was hard on both of us. Our workflow came to a pause and then a halt.

I had been friends with a community manager from Whitethorn Digital and asked her if she could do it and was interested in some of the job duties of PR. She had already been a champion of my work, and so it was such a great help. She did write-ups of my soundtrack for releases, edited a video with minimal footage and made introductions to podcasts to be featured on. Eventually, she stepped away from the role to manage her personal life. Nonetheless, she was great.

As I mention help, I would be remiss not to mention one of the best. She helped with all my graphics for some years, edited my photoshoot photos, introduced me to a great photographer, who is her best friend, designed my press kit and resume, did some write-ups for my press releases, designed mini marketing plans and near the end learned to edit my promo videos. It wasn't the smoothest collaboration, but hot damn, she was someone to behold in the composer's corner.

I still tried to determine what the universe was telling me about the problem. I felt I was being told to be patient and not try to force what I want. As creative as I was to shape someone into the role, which almost worked out, I still did not achieve the goal.

So, I decided to seek out other community managers and PR companies that work with independent games. You can tell by now that I've tried every which way to get this going but there was still some small frustration. My Mum calls it, "Step begging to be respected."

I have come to the point where I have discerned that I am my own best help. I have been operating this long so that I know the system and the most copacetic way to run it. I have figured out my shortcomings, come to peace with what was and what is and believe that I will finish what I have set to achieve. I am the "everyday help" but I am grateful to those that I have learned from and that help me in micro sporadic ways too. Every little bit counts.

22.4 JOURNALISM PRESS SIDEQUEST

I remember trying to pursue the angle to have a journalist write about my work. I was hell-bent on having the top IGN journalists of 2013–2017 care about what I was doing. Growing up seeing XPlay, it just seemed like a smart thing to do and an angle that no one else would take.

So, at GDC, I recall trying to get the attention of journalists that would be there because I know they would report about game industry news like PlayStation showing with their VR or Google Stadia.

I approached the top journalists at IGN (Max, Brian, Sam, Jared and Daemon). I was trying to pitch myself saying that I wrote music for this game, *I Can't Escape: Darkness*, to get them interested in it. I figured and thought people cared about the game and if I came with the angle of, I am a video game composer, they would be interested in someone that looked like me, who never approached them before versus them having to look for a story. I thought I was making it easy for them and that it was an indie game. From what I perceived from listening to the podcasts such as "BEYOND" and "Game Scoop" is that they "cared" about indie games but what I did not understand is that there was a bigger business going on.

The AAA games will always take precedence. So, as much as they personally do care about indie games and are interested, they have to do their job. Unless you are at a certain status and tier level in the industry, they will not "care" too much or if the game made a big splash that year overall and an impact sold millions of copies, got a loss of press, took off and went viral, it will not make a difference.

I used to search for validation from two journalists whom I respected for years. I remember meeting them at a couple of industry events, many times trying to work with them. I used to think that if I could achieve working with them, it would mean something but that never came to fruition. However, I did get close.

I almost wrote the music for a show they created and was recommended by an industry colleague who initially reached out to them to collaborate and got the gig. As he could no longer do the work due to starting a better position at a game company, I was introduced but the correspondence fell flat on their end (seems to be a pattern going on there in this field). So, I never succeeded in getting any of them interested in the work I did to write or share and eventually I gave up. I am glad I did. It was a very hard lesson to learn. I was doing something I said I would not do which was go against my name. This meant I was "chasing people".

So, when I realised it took a lot of energy to get their attention to regard my work as I had witnessed them do with other game composers at my level, and I was not getting anything back, I decided to re-alchemise that energy into myself. Eventually, more IGN articles came out, new people came into IGN, and they seemed interested in sharing my work. However, nothing has come from it yet. That is okay. What I learned is that I tried the sidequest and it didn't pan out. Yes, it was somewhat a waste of time, but I learned that it may not have been the best timing, and it was worth a try. The other lesson is that not all attention is created equal, no matter the level of rapport. I have to create my own attention for I am self-approved.

22.5 THE MAGFEST 2023 – 20TH YEAR EDITION (EXPERIENCE)

When I first heard about MAGFest, it was through an industry colleague. He and I met at my first GameSound Con in 2012. From there, I watched many acquaintances attend the illustrious MAGFest and post many photos online but since it always occurred in January, right after the holidays, I was pondering how many could afford going. I had hoped to attend one day.

FIGURE 22.3 MAGfest 13

However, hope is a placeholder. When you say you hope it's half of the belief in energy which leaves room for doubt. It's not concrete. This thought occurred for a decade until I started to believe that I would go someday and that's when something cool happened.

It all started when I got introduced to being a returning guest on Pixelated Audio.

FIGURE 22.4 Pixelated Audio – Chase Bethea PA-156 MAGWest 2021

Bryan and Gene asked me to come on as a guest in 2020 and I was happy to return. From there, I was introduced by Gene to the special guest coordinators of MAGWest and I was brought out to the event. It was fantastic and they loved working with me due to my professionalism. They asked me what I wanted from being a delight to work with and I requested to be brought out as a special guest to MAGFest 20th Year Edition, and it came to fruition a decade after I had first heard about the festival.

They treated me very well. They had a sign with my name held by a driver who picked me up in a black suburban truck. When I walked into the celebrity guest services, they knew my name even with a mask on. I entered my hotel room to find a gift basket with a note in a folder and a welcome note from the room service.

Biggest takeaway: Even with the level that I have reached, there are still not a lot of people who are familiar with my work. It's something I need to make an adjustment on to change.

This was a true sidequest. For years, I wanted to go to MAGFest and never knew how I would get out there. It's crazy how it all comes together. Here was the sidequest path.

FIGURE 22.5 MAGWest Sidequest Flow Chart

Return as a guest on a great video game music podcast>introduced to coordinator>get brought out to MAGWest>have a good work ethic that earns you a place as a special guest at MAGWest.

22.6 WINNING THE SECOND AWARD

This one is more a perspective of navigation.

"It sucks that you have to get kicked in the dick in order to transform the energy into what it made. Couldn't you just punch me in the arm?" – Efosa O.

This is what my best friend/brother said to me when I won my second NYX Award for Best Original Game Soundtrack for *On the Peril of Parrots.*

To go through so much pain in your personal life, sometimes it's hard to push through to make and more importantly complete art, especially when your professionalism is on the line. When you're in the mental abyss, you do not want to do anything. You do not want to sit with your thoughts, but you do not want to do any work, play any games, be social or move. For me, it was paralysing and every moment of that creation process felt like lifting 100 lbs up a mountain. So, when you manage to finish the art, submit it for an award and win, the retrospective kicks in. Questions formulate. "What kind of art would have been created if I did not feel that emotional pain? Would I have still won the award?" I believe this is what Efosa meant when he said being punched in the arm instead of the genitalia. As much as it sucked, a story was born, and the world received another historical piece of art to enjoy for our time.

22.7 MUSIC IMPRESSIONS TO LEGACY LEGEND

Sometimes, as I mentioned, you do side gigs, which can also be seen as sidequests, some of them can be very rewarding.

When I mixed Oran's last two tracks in March 2022, he asked if I had brought my music for him to listen to. I played him "Sleight Cliffhanger", music from *HEY POPS*, a game I was scoring for the Oculus at the time, which he loved the most, as he requested to play it twice. He also loved "Evaluations" and "Protector of Renar City" from the *Stardander School for Witches* Original Soundtrack and requested to play those twice as well. I exclaimed to him that my goal is to be one of the greatest in video game music history. He told me that "I am already that, all that needs to happen is for the world to wake up and see it."

A month later, on April 15, 2022, he said the game "Questlike Pocket" was incredible! When I initially played the music from that game for him along with the other tracks that day, he didn't say anything. However, I guess playing the game in context really changed his mind.

I did not seek or need the validation as I was already feeling rewarded by the universe to assist him with his music. He found me. He chose me. Nonetheless, I cannot deny the feeling of having your work be requested to be heard naturally by someone whose family comes from such a great legacy is in-explainable and humbling.

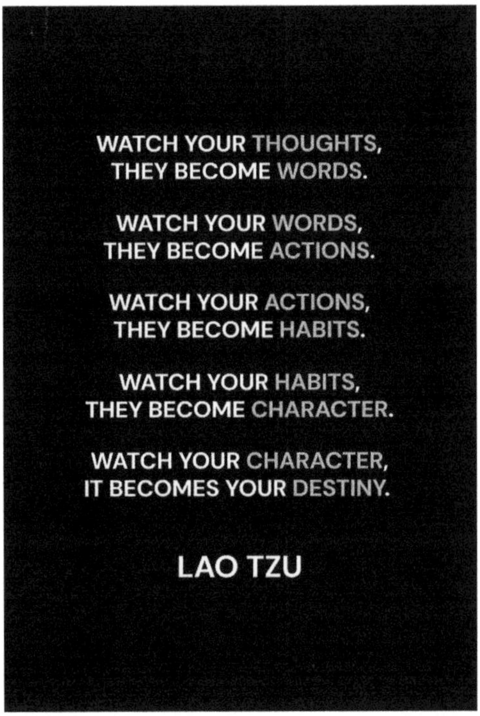

FIGURE 22.6 Watch Your Thoughts

My father had this pinned on his bulletin board when I was a child and during the many lectures that he gave me. He went over these words. During this time, I was 9 years old and the meaning and lesson to be taken from these words were not clear. However, once I became an adult and I revisited this, it all made complete sense.

As I apply this to my career and think back to the time when I decided to become a video game composer, I thought, "Yes, I can do this. I will do this." The words that came from my mouth when people asked what I do was, "I am an aspiring video game composer," because this is what the sentence everyone was saying. It was not until someone mentioned in a talk that once you have been paid for a gig, you are now a professional. The definition of "professional" will have many opinions from many but in this context, I define it to be paid for a service that delivers a product. So, the verbiage changed to "I am a professional video game composer" and I believed that. I thought and believed that if I could be paid and work on one game, I could do another and another. In turn, these became my actions.

I sought gig after gig after gig. I signed up for several game developer forums and looked for gigs every day for months. This became a habit. When I could not find gigs, I would sign up for game jams that interested me and the right amount of jam time (48 hours, 72 hours or one month). After a while, doing game jams became a habit too.

In turn, this rapidly built my portfolio and some of those game jams turned into paid projects and shipped titles. My work ethic with deliverables and communication was my character entering into games and

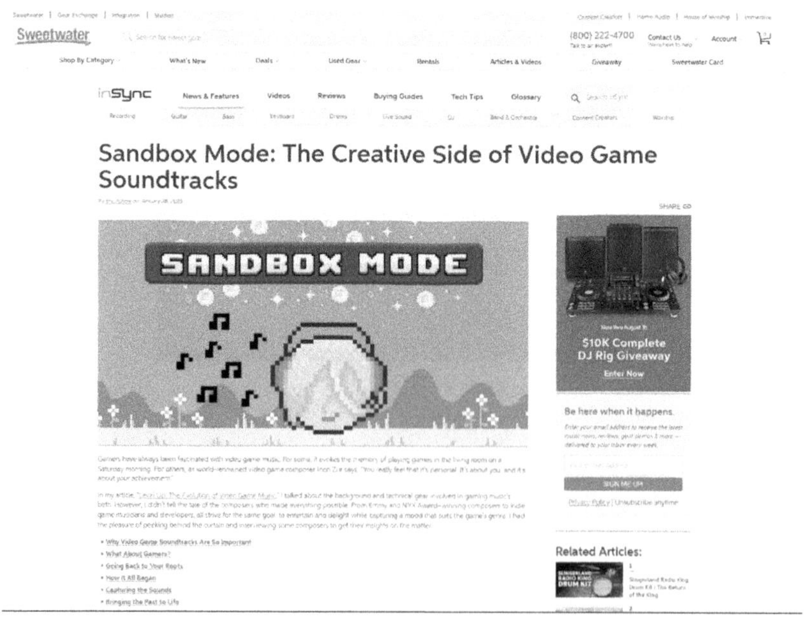

FIGURE 22.7 Sweetwater – The Sandbox Mode – The Creative Side of Video Game Soundtracks Article

becoming a reliable collaborator. I was able to establish true professionalism as a video game composer. This became another part of my character.

Through all of those actions and habits, my character became someone who is professional, creative, innovative, prolific and reliable. In addition, this propelled me to be discussed among other top professionals in my field.

22.8 SPEAKING AT BERKLEE COLLEGE – PART II

You never know where you will end up, so it pays to be nice. From Berklee College of Music asking me to be a guest speaker twice to Tom Salta saying

generated music using synth chips, MIDI, and samples. However, there has been a drastic shift. Because gear has become more easily accessible to the public, more composers now can record virtually anything they want or need and take advantage of hardware and software that wasn't available before.

In a recent interview, Zur, a Steinberg Cubase user, said that he didn't need the most expensive software. Each musician's workflow is different, so even having a few sound libraries on hand will help provide layers and layers until you can find the perfect sound.

Bethea, another Cubase user, not only utilizes unique instruments, like tabletop chimes and pan flutes, but he also works with software plug-ins, like the Roland ZENOLOGY, Ilio instruments, and the PluginGuru Unify.

How I Composed - "Concrete Rose" - Cubase to ELIAS

FIGURE 22.8 Sweetwater – The Sandbox Mode – The Creative Side of Video Game Soundtracks Article

that, "I got it," as an acknowledgement of my wisdom in my young years. I felt like the celebrity I always have felt I was. The room was packed and even though there weren't a lot of people afterwards to ask me questions as there was Tom, I still felt happy to be there and enjoyed the experience.

The outcome of all these experiences comes to the four P's. Presence, patience, passion and perseverance have been my pillars to navigate the video game industry in the past decade. With these four P's constantly in practice, I have incorporated them into my character and have achieved quite a bit but endured much more than I accounted for. Nonetheless, the combination has got me where I am today and could be the key to becoming the master of the game.

22.9 MISCONCEPTIONS

There seems to have been a huge misconception that took place in 2020, when I started showing up everywhere on people's feeds. People perceived me to be a mentor and thought I had figured things out. When, actually, I was just beginning to figure things out. Why is that? Why is it that no one had thought to ask me instead of assuming? Could it be based on my presence and presentation? How does one navigate through that misconception? I suppose for me I only took on what I could handle. I was offered many leadership roles but many of which I turned down. Had I been in a position to have long-term mentors who were always leading and properly *learn* how to be one as well as be more established in my career, then I may have accepted them. However, you don't always get to have the opportunities you wish to have, so later on, I took some leadership positions and went with the risk of learning along the way. An opportunity is an opportunity. It's what you make of it that it becomes something greater.

CHAPTER 23

Training Mode/ Experience Points (XP) – The Workout

When I started the workout, the goal was so I could fit my clothes again. I saw no point in buying new clothes. I was always unhappy with my look and my mental state. I had no idea my mentality would get a lot stronger to endure the future events in my life. I started training on January 21, 2021.

During the workouts, certain events such as BAFTA awards, G.A.N.G. awards and others that I submitted for occurred. Those awards went to the circle of nepotism and big-wallet companies. I was also overlooked by other opportunities.

The workouts helped me release the frustrations quicker and built a stronger mindset to endure. Eventually, I won one award, the NYX award, out of the seven I campaigned for.

I lost 20 lbs in one month without going to the gym. All exercises were done at home, and I did cardio daily. I adjusted my diet to no sugar and no bread. After that month, I was focused on maintaining and toning. That year, I worked out 340 days with only 25 days off.

Later on, I encountered some troublesome feelings in my personal life. I discovered that I avoid being uncomfortable and so I structured my workouts to be a little more difficult to push me into the mentality of being able to deal with it. This method of practice became useful even though

DOI: 10.1201/9781003422815-23

I did some of the exercises multiple times each day. It was still a struggle to reach the repetition and set goals comfortably. Nonetheless, I endeavoured, and the applications transferred seamlessly when encountered with personal contentions.

What I learned through these workouts was that thankfully it was an outlet for mental blocks I endured externally but also internally. At the beginning of the workout regimen, after I exercised, my mind was more open and creative than it had ever been before. I could think more rationally and clearly. I was more focused and could enact my plans with sharper acuity.

I'm grateful to discover the multiple benefits the exercise has brought me mentally. It's a life-changing experience that I shall continue henceforward.

During this period, I experienced some unsolicited criticism. During a workout, I ended up creating this small poem that summarised my response succinctly.

::Going Beyond::

Most people would see
The ambition I have is greed
It's really just an ingredient
In the recipe of growth
To level up my experience

The poem summarises the focus and initiative that I practice daily. With every breath and every opportunity that we wake up, we have the choice to be better as humans and evolve. I strive to be the best and healthy version of me I can be to myself while balancing my HP, replenishing my mana and ascending with clear energy.

CHAPTER 24

Developer Collaboration Experiences

Some developers who have never worked with game audio people at a certain calibre don't know how to communicate that well. I experienced that some indie developers who have done a lot of the work on their project alone have some of these shortcomings.

I found that some developers who have made music but are more active and proficient at game design, level design and programming are a little more difficult to communicate the musical idea to. I would think that since they have actually made music before, there would be an understanding of what the composer does for musical choices for the game. However, the nitpick slows the process down. I believe that the developer should trust the composer to do the work you hired them for. If they are really off path with the work, run it past some other people to see if they hear and have the same opinion first before explaining yourself.

Working with Idan from Drimia Interactive [*Aztec Ride*]. Idan is an Israeli developer. After shipping *Aztec Ride* on mobile, he was silent since I sent him the contract for the track I composed for *Aztec Ride*. I reached out via Discord message and inquired if he had any funding or winnings from the pot from the game. Idan proceeded to phone me and he sounded really excited to hear from me too. He said, "No but we get lots of articles written about us." I had thought that when we got the news that we won the BIG Indie Pitch, there would be at least $1200. However, apparently, there was "no money". We only received promotional press. So, since it

DOI: 10.1201/9781003422815-24

was a game jam game and there was no income, the contract became obsolete. At least that got squared away. Then, he asked how I was doing.

We had a really good chat. As I followed him on social media, I saw he was also releasing a bunch of games. Idan mentioned that at the time, those games were for school and that he had to finish for the semester. He is really cool, so he might be busy, but he is still down to Earth, and we have a good relationship and I helped him out with a couple of resource videos. I shared some marketing insights with him and suggested that he put his game on Steam because he was leaving money on the table. He's made some money from the small releases of his other games and he's really good at promoting them.

So, we each had some value to offer each other. I think Idan is a good person to keep up with, especially since we worked well together on *Aztec Ride* and we got along. The lesson is that sometimes connections strengthen through phone conversations. I have thought of this experience often as I have gone forward.

Other development teams trust their composer but may reach other limitations. However, optimism can overcome obstacles.

24.1 IT'S THE LITTLE THINGS

Initially, when joining the project, I talked to the team about having dynamic music.

A year into development, the rest of the team mentioned they probably would not be able to implement that feature. In addition, ELIAS, the audio middleware company, was going through a transition. So, I proceeded to make normal game loops.

However, at one music meeting in September 2023, one of the dev team members mentioned having the "time period of 60s/70s". I knew I could achieve this by adding a filter and using iZotope Vinyl.

So, I wrote the loop, but it occurred to me that there was a dynamic music opportunity. I came up with the idea to render the loops with three options.

Option 1: "filter_only" indicating the low end (bass line) is being heard along with other instruments.

Option 2: "filter_and_vinyl" – the low end (bass line) is no longer there due to the effect of the time period.

Options 3: "non-filtered" – no filters at all, "high-fidelity".

From the game design idea aspect and possible monotony break, this could add some dynamic/interactive variety to be used in certain sections of the game.

I suggested if we used the non-filtered version of the photo album music for one act, go to some marginalia scenes and come back to the photo album. Then, we can use the "filter_and_vinyl" version as an option. It came down to experimentation, but it could work.

The programmer complimented my work by saying, "Thank you for lining up the times of the different versions perfectly – it's so satisfying getting to swap from one [music file] to the other at the same time point."

I am glad that it worked. I knew that all the three music file options were to be rendered at the same lengths because the arrangement time doesn't change, just the effect which I enabled and disabled.

So, to my surprise, as I played the latest Adventure X build, I had seen compliments about the music changing between scenes. As I played, I noticed the "Late Blues Party" music was used from "filter_and_vinyl" and finally "non_filtered" before changing to the photo album scene. The music occurs and fades in seamlessly with the text. Dynamic music is achieved on a basic level with no middleware. This is a semi-planned happy accident and huge win! It proves I knew the core concepts of interactivity and when explained correctly can be implemented. More importantly, it's subtle and effective. It's the little things. Compliments to the team programmer for trying out my idea and taking the experimentation further.

CHAPTER 25

Strategy Guide

Many composers have asked me over the years what are my strategies to overcome composer writer's block. I've shared a few of these but not the full list until now.

Take Time Away. Simple things such as washing dishes, going for a walk, tending to a garden, cleaning a car and going on a mini trip for a few days help. This allows your brain to separate briefly, return refreshed and with better focus.

Do Something Else that Is Related. Listen to some music that a friend recommended that you have been putting off or a piece of music you have been delaying. Also, practicing and/or learning a repertoire piece. What should happen when you play the piece is that your mind focuses on the new music and you may hear something while playing that you may like that "inspires" you. I can't express how much this has helped me.

During my time at Moorpark College, I was in the Applied Program. This program selected the best students who exhibited talent and potential to be nurtured by proficient instructors. Only 15 students were selected per calendar year, and they were for multiple instruments: Voice, Cello, Piano and Guitar. A truly elite program. Within this program, the students are given repertoire to perform at an upper university level. So, by playing that difficult repertoire, I was exposed to new musical ideas I typically would not have been introduced to otherwise.

DOI: 10.1201/9781003422815-25

Copy Other Work to Study Only. Do Not Publish It. This method is strictly for learning purposes. Try to emulate someone else's style you like. I had to learn how to do this in Uni. In film scoring class, they had us copy the styles of Jerry Goldsmith, Danny Elfman, Thomas Newman, Marco Beltrami and John Williams of pre-written scores from specific films. I personally found this process to be very difficult, especially emulating John Williams (surprisingly, I received high remarks on that one). However, I learned how the "BIG BOYS" composed for that media. As I talked to other peers, I learned from a few Jazz students that they had transcribed certain solos from prominent Jazz musicians. When I watched them do it, my takeaway was that they became better soloists when I saw them perform at various recitals. My transcription skills were already strong since fifth grade as I used to do that during Saxophone practice. I became bored practicing my band music so much and other warm-up pieces such as "Hot Cross Buns" for homework. So, I would turn on WNUA 95.5 (an old Smooth Jazz radio station that used to air in Chicago) and transcribe certain Saxophone parts. The inspiration is very close to you. You just have to listen.

Refer to Old Ideas. If you had an idea that was festering before in an old session that you did not finish, open it and look for small motivic themes and/or textures that you can use with fresh ears, you may hear differently. This has come in handy for me on some occasions. Why should I force myself to write something new when my past self already did? I just need to add on to what I started. In these cases, it has saved me time and sometimes turns out to be the jump start I needed to get the creativity flowing.

Sing. The act of singing can spawn a plethora of ideas. It's an interesting phenomenon. This one I do the most and has got me through a lot of writer's block, especially when writing the music for *Aground*. I normally would combine two or three of the methods that I have already listed. One time, I referred to an old idea, got up, started washing dishes (taking time away) and hummed/sang. I did small intervallic exercises, and some musical ideas came to me.

Refer to Track Ideas. Do you have melodies that come to you in your dreams? I do. I immediately force myself out of sleep and record them. This has come in handy many times. Have you been in a grocery store and heard a faulty wheel on a shopping cart and it makes an odd rhythm? I have and it's helped with starting a track in *Aground*. Inspiration is all around us but most of the time if you don't look for it, it will come to you. When it does, capture the moment on your phone or portable recorder (if you carry one of those). Then, refer to it later when you get stuck. It's clutch.

Release Limitations. Try to play on instruments that you are not familiar with. Tinker. Experiment. For example, I have a Kalimba that I cannot play very well but when I play around with it, I remember that it is still music, and I am unlocking something within myself that is supposed to be made.

Improvise. This technique is probably the most effective of them all. I cannot tell you how many times this has come in handy. I've written two-minute pieces based on improvisation for games. One of them is on the *Electron Flux* Original Soundtrack ("W Induction" – Main Theme). When I do not know what I want to do, I just hit record and play. 9/10 times I use what I recorded the first time. It works well when the self-management isn't functioning that day as much as you had hoped it would. There is something about this process that allows the mind to be in a fluid state. I don't overthink. I don't correct mistakes. I just play. When I like what I did then, I record it. It's fast, simple and liberating.

FIGURE 25.1 Kalimba + Flute

Start with Two Measures. Nowadays, I start with four measures so that I can at least complete a phrase or motif. There is something alleviating about writing two measures. I think the psychology behind this is that it is similar to an English composition writing technique I learned at Moorpark College from my professor Mr. McGee. He said, "If you can write two sentences, then, you can write four. If you can write one page, you can write ten. If you can write ten pages, you can write a hundred." At first, this sounded ridiculous to me, but my professor was right and as I progressed in college, I was writing bigger papers, and the process began to be easier. So, when we were told we had to write a 25-page paper, my peers freaked out and I thought to myself, "Piece of cake!" This concept to break down the bigger picture down to a minute goal was more attainable than thinking, "I have to write a four-minute piece." It's more mentally digestible to sit and write two measures, no matter how much time you have or don't have. In addition, what should happen, if you allocate the time to write two measures, is the state where you get in the zone and you will write beyond two measures. Once this state enacts, the writer's block will become no more.

Read a Music Production Magazine. Oh man. Either magazines are dated, or no one reads anymore. Well, hopefully you are still reading this book to learn about this tip. Over the years, I have discovered a plethora of music production tips. I have come across different sample processing styles, plugins that colour mixes and DAW workflows. Although the information was not directly what I was seeking, remaining optimistic allowed my curiosity to become experimental and led me to some interesting finds. I'll leave it here and hopefully it sparks an interest to begin sourcing through tons of material.

Ask a Non-Musician Friend to Critique Your Music. Choose someone that you respect, trust but that does not play or has ever played an instrument but has a good ear for music, their opinion and feedback on whatever you have written so far. I understand that this person may possibly be hard to find in the beginning, but you probably know at least a few people who fit this description already who can help you. Based on the constructive criticism, it should push you to finish the track. Complete the process from the beginning of writing to the end of the composition process, allowing them to hear the music as you get over the blocks.

Dictation. Hopefully, you did this in Uni already. If you're like me, this was a weakness, and I had to put extra hours of practice in to get a passing grade. By the time I was in Musicianship VI, I had learned to love dictation so much that I found it to be a very useful tool to overcome the writer's barrier. I recommend doing the following:

Rhythmic Dictation. This is the base of music. Without this, melodies are not strong, and chord progressions can be stale.

Melodic Dictation. You are sure to find some inspiration by doing a few of these. If you add the other technique I mentioned before, singing, you might come up with something that you like.

Harmonic Dictation. This is my personal favourite. As I begin to transcribe, my inner ear takes over and I get into it. I get great satisfaction from hearing and dictating the correct chord progressions played from root position to all inversions and qualities.

Intervallic Dictation. I believe this one is the hidden gem. It can be the spark of a motif that can turn into a strong melody once you do a few rounds of it. They are short, sweet and just enough to tickle the musical imagination.

Time Palette Listening. This method is one that combines a multitude of tips that I mentioned earlier. I have found this to be a higher training of transcription. First, you turn on the radio and/or pick a playlist you don't know and then pick apart the song and write everything you hear in one listen (i.e. chord progressions, rhythms, melodies, countermelodies, song forms, etc.). Not only have I found that this sharpens all of the skills I practice individually but a weird phenomenon occurs, where I hear one thing in the song that piques my interest and sets me down the experimental writing path. When the next song comes on, I do the same process again. Even if I do not find anything inspiring in one song, if I do the exercises a few times, I am bound to find something that I can tinker with.

Use a Friend's Phone Number as a Chord Progression. I've never heard someone come up with this before and I have read a lot of music theory books. So, I am coining this now as the "Bethea Theory". Once you determine the key signature and tempo. If you are stuck on choosing a key signature, then use a friend's name. How many letters are in their name? Seven? Well, pick a 7/4-time signature.

Now, let's say my friend's phone number is "324–5936". I know the first question some of you may be asking is, "What do I use for the zeros?" Make it a wild pick. Choose an augmented sixth chord (Neopolitan, Fr6, It6 or Ger 6 or whatever Sus chord). The "9" in the phone number is an interchangeable interval. 2/9 and 9/2. We have two "3s" in the phone number. We can substitute one for a number we don't have. We don't have a tonic, so let's change out the last "3" for a "1" and make the chord progression a deceptive cadence. Now, we have a chord progression. For this example, I chose a minor key so the roman numerals will reflect that and I'm going to use some borrowed chords too. "iii, flat II, iv, V, ii (half-diminished), i, vi".

Depending on the phone number you choose, you may have to alter more numbers to make a chord progression you like. The point of the exercise is to get you unstuck. If you decided on a key signature and already indited a chord progression, you should have unblocked yourself by now. Plus, you can tell your friend, "Hey, you're sort of in my music that is in this game!" They may be surprised and honoured to know that you were inspired by their phone number to make a music chord progression.

25.1 OPPORTUNITIES I WISH I HAD – OPPORTUNITIES I DID HAVE – OPPORTUNITIES I HANDLED WRONG

Choosing the clients/people you want to work with. I read this on the "Career Guide" website back in 2010–2011 and I had applied to a few big game companies. The ruse of getting hired at these companies straight out of college for someone like me was a lie. I only wish that when I was meeting developers at GDC (Game Developers Conference), I had applied the methodology sooner to build my portfolio. In a sense, I was doing that but not with the same mentality focus approach.

I did this with the game, *Twelve Minutes*. I found the developer sitting at a table by himself at IndieCade back in 2013. He was working on his game. At the time, he was the art director of The Witness. When I saw the game, I knew it was a gem and that it would take off. I kept in touch with him for many years. For one IndieCade, I even bought him lunch on the first day and helped him at his booth by watching it so that he could get lunch the second day. It was a genuine volunteering gesture. He didn't have any help. I really wanted to be the composer of the game but in 2016, I was offered a test for sound designer, and I got the gig. I was the first sound designer that worked on the game. What I did not take into consideration was personality fit.

Throughout the years of communication with him, it was a good, cordial conversation. In the industry, the saying is, "People hire their friends". On the other hand, there's a saying that goes, "Never work with your friends". The developer and I had built trust. We didn't hang out, but I showed deep interest and belief in *Twelve Minutes* and that trust led me to being able to do a small collaboration. However, once you work with people, you get to see another side of them that normally happens once you collaborate. There was a clear personality mismatch in work styles and communication. As disheartening as it was to me, I could only blame myself for not thinking that was a possibility that could occur before accepting the gig. I had pursued this game for close to five years and I lost the passion for being on the project within two months. I had high hopes and a false perception that being on the project would define my place in the industry and lead to even bigger projects. Alas, I was wrong, but it was an imperative learning experience that I will never forget.

If I had known not to have tunnel vision of what the project could do for me, I might have thought of the personality concept. Maybe if someone told me. Maybe if the universe had let me know in some blatant way. However, that didn't happen. The experience was meant for me to learn a lesson, so I believe it happened for a reason. Perhaps it was for me to share with you as the reader what I know now.

25.2 ATTRIBUTE ALLOCATION ASSESSMENT CHECK – EDIT MODE

I noticed a lot of new generation composers are just looking for handouts and answers to get advice from anyone and everyone that will get them to the road to success the fastest. That's not exactly the best approach because, in my opinion, you don't know who you are, and you will be unable to describe to others your story of how you reached that level of success. Frankly, it's boring. You can do better, and you should! The cliche phrase I constantly hear is, "The world and no one owes you anything". However, I believe if you care about the impact you want to have on others, then you owe it to yourself to be the best human you can be in the world. Start by consistently doing your homework about the field. Regardless of whether something is relevant, continue to do your industry research. The best thing that can happen is you gain knowledge about the history of the industry. This arms you with how and where you fit into this big space. It will take you far. Applied knowledge is power.

> Everyone has their goals, priorities and objectives. These may not coincide however, you must find ways to provide value to those you seek assistance from. In the past decade I have rarely asked for favors, and I have never asked for a favor unless I am bringing equal value to them. I do not offer what I think might be valuable to them based on their own priorities but something I know to be valuable to them. I care to do my due diligence. I don't hypothesize on what they might need. I do research, I listen, and I provided solutions.
>
> – CLINTON SPARKS

Skill-Strengthen Your Social Skills. I worked in retail for ten years. This was the best thing I could do to build my interpersonal skills. It taught me about customer service. I learned many lessons about respecting others of all creeds and cultures. Most importantly, I gained valuable intellect on how to interact with multiple personalities at any given moment at a professional level.

Skill-Stay Humble is a lesson that I was raised on by my great-grandmother, Laurie Brewster, since I was 7 years old. I came into this industry seeing some people gassed up on their own egos. It was very deflating and as I watched some peers and colleagues who started out around the same time I did, rise in ranks, job positions and popularity, I also saw the same hot air balloon egos inflate. I was sharp. Staying humble no matter what level of success you reach has brought longevity to those I admire in many industries: Basketball, Tech, Music, Film/TV, Marketing and more. What I have seen is that those egos got popped from their own self-inflation. You can be on the high but manage your air levels.

Skill-Treat Everyone at All Levels of Their Respective Career with Genuine Courtesy. There is a big, nasty attitude I have seen grow from many newcomers. They ask the infamous question, "What game(s) have you worked on?" If you don't mention the hot ticket ones like *Halo*, *Destiny*, *Call of Duty*, *Last of Us*, *Journey* or *Horizon Zero Dawn*, then they immediately check out and dismiss you. Rookie mistake! You just burned a potential friendship that could lead to many more ways than just a gig. But if that's the mindset that you wish to have for a good way to "network", then please carry on.

What I have seen from veterans is that they want to see if you can think for yourself and work hard. They don't care too much about the projects you scored or sound design assets you made. Do you have the mental sustainability to run a marathon? Some of the veteran pros (not all) are like wolves and they smell blood. They have the foresight to see the potential in you before you even approach them. So be cognizant of your actions and how you carry yourself. You're always being watched.

You're not going to connect with everyone and not everyone is going to like you. The best approach is to be yourself and those who want to connect and genuinely befriend you will. This is not easy to do. You will go through a mental process, but you have the ability to allow quality into your life.

25.3 [DEBUG/PRACTICE MODE]

So, I have often been asked how to manoeuvre from doing work in college to becoming an industry professional. Here is what I did. I designed the three-stage system of getting started from college to professional level. I believe that if we follow this tier system that I helped create along with my game developer friend, Clifton B, we can create healthier bids and possibly, over time, eviscerate free/exploited work on professional projects.

We as freelance composers are either supposed to be charging by the minute or per asset. What I was running into with independent developers is that they want AAA quality products but aren't budgeting properly for this. This is in some way forcing some of us as audio creative professionals to live below our means and fight against other creatives who will offer to do it for nothing. Credit is good and frankly, should be a given, but credit doesn't put a roof over our head or food on the table. So, if the "Indie Rate" for music is at the minimum \$500 per finished minute and you have someone who has been nominated in the industry or won a few awards, shipped several games on multiple platforms, and lives in a city that's somewhat expensive or not, then you can estimate that their rate is at least \$1000 per finished minute (minimum). Those costs go into almost all of what was listed on the photo above, depending on the type of music.

For sound designers, it's the same. In the book *The Complete Guide to Game Audio* by Aaron Marks, the second edition illustrates that when you start out, SFX are \$25.00 per sound effect. At some point, you should reach \$50.00, and this second edition was published in 2009. Add ten years of inflation and you can estimate what the rate per sound effect should be now.

When a new composer who was starting in the industry asked me at GDC four years ago what I charged for SFX, I told him $75.00 per SFX, and he squawked at me. He said I charged more than someone he was working with. To me, that was way low considering my experience, and I felt I was being magnanimous. I calmly debated and factored my cost of living, talent and experience versus theirs. I also conducted my best research about what the new rates were to be competitive.

25.4 STAGE 1: BEGINNING EDUCATION – JUST LEARNING

25.4.1 Game Jams

Do game jams, game jams, game jams. I always mention this in the plethora of podcast interviews I do. This is where you learn to make mistakes. You may not realise it but the jams that you take part in change your life in a good way. You learn about how to explore your limits and discover new ideas that will hopefully electrify your creativity. Jamming is the place where you break out of your comfort zone to also and hopefully make new friends and/or new experiences with familiar ones.

Here you can make the best of the opportunity. Be open to all ideas and those who wish to collaborate with you.

I want to make something very clear. Game jams are not about crunch. It's about learning your limits. Yes, you have a brief amount of time to make something but the only pressure you have is upon yourself. This is the time to learn how to practice, pace, strengthen communication and critical listening skills and quality assurance with assets for context. This is where you learn so many things. If you are thinking about going into game development as a career, that is where you can take the opportunity to see what goes into it. At the end of the jam, you will be able to assess if you wish to pursue it or have it be a hobby. Jams are also used to learn new techniques, software and experiment with an idea that has been lingering in the back of your brain. Use the time you would not have made any other day to learn some new technology to use in the jam if you feel it will not stress you or the team out. Once you begin, you'll find out very quickly if it's daunting and time-consuming or if you are good at it.

Remember, no one is going to lay you off, shut down your studio, or revoke investments if you don't get your game to the state of what you envisioned it to be. Game jams should be perceived to be the best starting point. Create to play and if you get more done or even finish the game, then that is icing on the cake.

FIGURE 25.2 Global Game Jam 2016 Theme Reveal

Game jams make opportunities. Over the years, we have seen so many successful game titles that were born from Global Game Jam such as *Keep Talking and Nobody Explodes*, *How to Do It* and more. Some games have spawned successful game studios. Those studios have created jobs

FIGURE 25.3 Global Game Jam 2016 – Slide

for people to get their start in the game industry, earn a living and build a career and do what they love to do, make games. I owe most of my career to game jams. If it wasn't for these, I would have struggled a lot more to get a portfolio started and even get work in the field. I sometimes game jam to this day because it's the best way to tap into my childhood creativity. Something I think is lost as we grow up. But it's still there, we just have to dig deep into game jams, which are the perfect time to scoop it up.

During this educational period, I highly suggest game jams – These jams are the greatest way to get started. If you can't find game jams to be a part of, then get involved with mods. Mods are an awesome build your portfolio and who knows, it may become something bigger such as *Dota 2, Garry's Mod or Black Mesa.*

Keep in mind, if these are hobby games, part of a jam or side project, on a team you helped form, it's appropriate to work without compensation *at your discretion* – because you're working for yourself and for the experience. Outside of this scenario, even if you'd consider yourself a Tier 1 designer, if someone recruits you to help with a game, you're now doing

FIGURE 25.4 Global Game Jam 2016 Space

a service for them. You're a professional who deserves to be paid for your time and effort.

Mods – Here is where you can gain some more experience. Games like *Black Mesa* and *Dota 2* have created many opportunities for people to

FIGURE 25.5 Bushido Bots – Waking Oni

learn and build solid portfolio pieces. Some Mods have turned into careers for people.

Student Projects from Art Institute and Other Art Programs – With a little research, one can find a plethora of student projects to be involved in doing game audio. Sometimes, these projects turn into bigger projects if the programmer/team decide to expand the game and either look for funds on Kickstarter/Indie-a-gogo or release it commercially and split the revenue share. This also works well for student composers who are learning. You work with peers and build early relationships that may grow into professional ones should both of you continue to pursue your creative ambition in the industry.

25.5 STAGE 2: NEAR THE END OF EDUCATION/ CLOSE TO GRADUATION

Here is where you have received enough knowledge about your craft that you can start charging for your services. Near the end of this process, when you are a year from graduation is when it would be safe to start charging or trading for services. It's a super good time to think about a website and logo. Brainstorm now! If they cannot pay you, work out a trade of services for something you need. It's only fair. By now, you should have enough portfolio pieces for potential clients to speculate if your skills are right for the project.

By this time, you should be properly educated on what the industry rates are, and if you're not, you should begin researching immediately. The goal is to remain competitive. Do not work for nothing. You cannot expect people with qualifying experience to work for nothing. It's disrespectful.

There is a common issue that is circulating rapidly on the Internet about "working for free". Many new musicians want to break into the game industry so badly that they are willing and are doing free work. This creates a huge imbalance between the professionals and the newcomers which doesn't help the industry, in fact it becomes a hindrance and will diminish our growth if it continues.

There needs to be a clear definition of what kind of game audio person/musician decides to be, a professional or a hobbyist. Separating yourself can allow the professional to bid appropriately, as well as create healthy competition for the longevity of our industry. The professionals will not have to figure out how to compete with "free" work when the person next to you is using the same equipment. In the same respect, as a hobbyist, if you do it for the "love of the game" and just for fun, then that should be specified and also targeted in non-professional. If at some point, the hobbyist decides to do game audio for a living, then they should charge competitive rates and take the necessary steps to be a professional in the industry. There is a clear line between game audio professionals who are doing it for a living/love it and those that just do it for fun. Identify yourself.

Like everything in this world, it takes money to make money and game development is no different. Video games are another form of software development and therefore require tools to make quality professional assets and content. Yes, most software to make games is cheap and/or free but there is still some sort of threshold that exists that separates the professionals from the hobbyists.

Learning the basics while you are in school should help you keep learning by yourself. I suggest you start charging "indie rates" to get familiar with those who value you, your time, talent and craft. You'll be able to discern very early those who don't want to pay. Please research what the current rates are.

We don't see this happening in other industries that much. Starbucks doesn't make its coffee free to compete with Peets or Coffee Bean or other mom and pop coffee shops. Construction workers don't work for free when other construction companies have better rates. They may offer a discount here and there but that's it. Our services should be no different.

As creatives, we invest 10k plus hours of practice, countless hours of studying the craft, going to school, and applying for school grants and loans. We pay for quality plugins and software for the music to sound good for future players to enjoy. When in your mind did someone tell you it was free? When did bills stop? When did you become entitled? You must charge for your work. Especially in the age of AI.

AI itself will not make our work obsolete but the people using AI who did not value music in the first place will use it to make our work less valuable, which may make our jobs as video game composers non-existent. Until they wake up and realise that humans buy and play their games. Humans are their audience, and they also have bills to pay just like we do. This is out of our control for that awakening but what is in our control is to charge competitively not cheaply, for the work we do because it's a lot. We don't just have to learn to write music, we have to know how to implement, learn code and learn middleware. This costs time and money. If most developers do not see you as part of a team, then you need to function like a proper service provider. If you do not know how to do that, start researching and learning. It does not just benefit all creatives, but it benefits you in the short term and long term.

Do your research and homework about what the current standard rates are and add 10% to them. Stand your ground on the price. Your work will speak for itself, and they will pay for it. Be open to negotiating options that are nominally fair to both parties. Always be willing to walk away if the terms are not fair.

If you are participating in a game jam, this may be the time you do not get paid. However, even game jams have cash prizes sometimes. Most developers do not care about music because they can get it cheap and for free. If you're not serious about adding value to this industry, do not waste your time. You're only hurting and damaging the field more. If you choose not to invest in yourselves, others will not invest in you.

Before you graduate, you should have at least two paying clients. I suggest not having as many services for trade so that you can get an understanding of how to operate as a freelancer. If you're seeking to be an employee at a game studio and not a freelancer, then what I previously said does not apply to you.

Try to get paid something and if the client approves to share a proper percentage (5%–20%) of revenue shares from the game sales, then that will help as well to make up for your rate costs if they cannot meet the field rates. As you have been reading by now, every person's mentality is different, so hopefully they will be able to negotiate with you and come to fair terms that benefit both sides.

When I was in community college, by the time I was in my third year/fourth music theory class, which was the last theory class offered at the institution, I had decided that I was going to work in games before it got over-saturated. That was my exact thought. The book *The Complete Guide to Game Audio* by Aaron Marks helped me ship my first game without any direct mentorship, internship or apprenticeships. I had landed my first paid gig and shipped my first game as a student before I graduated from Moorpark College.

By the time I attended California State University, Northridge [CSUN] I was nominated in the entire industry for VGMO (Video Game Music Online) Artist of the Year – Best Independent Composer among the other nominees, Chipzel ("Interstellaria"), Shaun Chasin ("Hektor"), Kyohei Fujita ("dreeps"), Soshi Hosoi ("Otaku Circle's Princess"), David Housden ("Volume"), Jack Menhorn ("Nova-111") and Keiji Yamagishi ("Exile's End") and was receiving royalties from at least two games I worked on.

I share this to show that it is possible to have a few if not more paid gigs as a freelancer in games before graduating Uni.

25.6 STAGE 3: SELF-SUFFICIENT – MAKING MONEY TO LIVE

By this time, you have shipped at least one game on PC, Mobile, or Console. You have graduated and you SHOULD BE charging for your work. The saying in the industry is "You can work for free, but don't work for nothing." If at all possible, try to follow that but always, always try to get paid SOMETHING first. You are self-sufficient and are making money to live to be a professional. You have expenses like everyone else and deserve to be compensated for your time, skill, talent and hard work. Asus computers, software plugins and synthesiser keyboards don't grow on trees, and your school loan is collected every month just as much as that of a programmer or artist.

Some Exceptions to system

1. Friend or friend of a friend's passion project – There is nothing wrong doing a solid for a good friend. It builds rapport. Maybe just take each other to lunch to show appreciation for the time given or a trade in creative skills works just as well.

2. Your own project. If all else fails, make something small yourself. I have heard quite a few success stories where people did this and landed a job in the industry. It shows that you take initiative and can complete a product with discipline.

There are alternatives to getting to work on games besides working for free or nothing on semi-commercial projects.

Here are a few jobs you can do as a freelancer that revolve around music.

Instruct Instrument Lessons. I was told by a field colleague that this was "sustainable". However, my experience has shown otherwise, and I have heard from others who have instructed before that it's not as stable as one may think. For the most part, it's better to be seen as a gig rather than a part-time or full-time job unless you work at an institution. Many parents cancel or try to take advantage of the lessons, many children don't practice, and this can be debilitating, and if they are private lessons, some may not pay on time. Instruct because you love it and those things I mentioned may not bother you.

Orchestrate and/or Arrange Music. This skill can come in handy for other composers who may be in use of this. Many make a good living doing this type of work, sometimes on the side or full-time. If you have some solid clients, this can be a semi-sustainable gig while you build your composing music career. It also strengthens your chops for your own compositions.

A/V Tech Work. I think this is a cool opportunity. You get to meet other musicians and possibly some good friendships that will lead to more work. It also gets you away from the house/computer and keeps you physically active. You know I'm an advocate for this. It provides some stability depending on where you live and offers a nice balance between the financial seasons.

Imagine being on the other side of the table or being in other people's shoes and you are hiring for audio to sell your game. Would you want the potential game player that you want to buy your game to undervalue your hard work that you did all the time by pirating it? When they do that, they are essentially getting it for free, and if many people do this, the industry value of games falls or many game developers give their games away for free just to get people to play. This also damages the economics of the field. What you don't want to do is make people think it much less than what it is. When you are constantly discounting your services, it gives people the perception that your time, talent and hard work is not worth much.

25.7 SEEING PEOPLE AS YOUR FRIENDS AND EQUALS

There are so many games and so many people willing to pay for games that it's more beneficial to you to help your friend get a job, so you will not lose out on one. Empathising with people, realising that they need help too. Try not to see others as competition because there are so many jobs out there, we should not be at each other's throats. When I was speaking to some of my game designer friends, they shared that they have never met other game designers and have been like "grrrr, I'm [also] a game designer." However, what I have sometimes seen and experienced is that when other audio professionals meet each other, typically composers, they have this instant ego or arrogance. There is definitely no need for it. It's a "crabs in a bucket" mentality that should be rethought.

25.8 DOING STAGE WORK RATE BASIS

In relation to where you are, either Stage 1, Stage 2 or Stage 3, charging per project will most likely be best at this stage. Small teams do not want to think about a "blank check" they may have to write. Once you get the attention of the AAA studios, they are usually the ones that can write those types of checks and you can choose to transition, if the studio permits to charge per hour. If something isn't done right, then it takes hours to fix, and more money comes from the client. It's unfortunate but it is part of the job and the territory.

This "stage" system should give some structure to transitioning from being a student to working professionally.

25.9 THE LOST LEVEL

It's ironic really because audio is what really sticks with people. A lot of game developers do not give it that much focus because they think it is only the visuals that matter. However, the player/consumer can and will recognise this.

one of the beta testers had as their first bullet point why they liked the game (after not expecting much):

> The soundtrack - From the moment I clicked onto the game I could hear good quality music. Not many game developers put the effort into adding quality soundtracks in their games, and instead use some poorly made music that sounds like it was made by a beginner, but this game showed me the opposite.

FIGURE 25.6 Beta Tester from *Aground* Message

To both parties, especially for developers, when you ask for rates, you need to start to learn to present numbers first. Everything is negotiable. Try to stop being afraid to share what you would like to spend on the audio budget. We will both save time on having to go through the rigmarole of guessing what the number is. This is exhausting and inefficient. You obviously know what you want to spend, and the audio professional will likely know their rate. If you can't meet that for the prospective contractor, then allow them to counter offer. Too many developers are all so quick to disappear and not have a proper dialogue. If you're not interested in bartering, then verbally say "No, thank you" and then exit. Remember, you represent yourself and your brand. The social tunnel goes both ways. So, word will travel, like it does about us as freelancers, of how unprofessional you and/or your studio are and how we should not work with you.

Message to new freelance game audio professionals: Charge what you're worth. What does that mean? That means figuring out your expenses for car insurance, car notes, rent/mortgage, utility bills, groceries, gas, health insurance and everything you need to live. Figure out how much time it takes to write all genres of music. Hit the stopwatch as soon as it starts and stay off the social media and ignore text messages until it's done. If you MUST respond to someone, stop the stopwatch and log your time to stay consistent, when you start again. If you need certain equipment or software for the gig, calculate that in your quote. This is a part of your rate. Stand up for yourself and ask for it. If they can't afford you, then it's not the right client and unfortunately, we will have to do something in the interim that we may not want to do in order to meet that client who will pay your rate someday. But a client who will not pay your worth is not worth your time, talent and effort. Just like in a relationship, if that person you're dating or your partner is not going to show you respect, consistency and reciprocation for the time, love and effort you put into the relationship, you should walk away. They do not value your worth and you have to be alone sometimes until you want to find, or someone finds you and will value your worth.

An excerpt from *The Complete Guide to Game Audio* by Aaron Marks (emphasis added):

> In the beginning, it is very tempting to give away your art for free, in order to add a project to your resume. But what it does instead is let a game developer take advantage of you and **cheapen our**

> **profession**. At the *least*, make sure your expenses are paid. While the rush of creating music for your first game can invigorate your soul, it will be short-lived when you have to sell some of your equipment to pay the rent. It's just not worth doing it for free. Your talent adds value to a product they will sell and make a lot of money from. Make sure to receive your fair share as an integral part of the team who put it together.

It's okay to ask for trades! If they can't pay your rate for that gig, then ask for some equipment or software that will help you get a leg-up on the current gig or next gig. This is working for something not nothing. The majority of the time, the client will actually pay for it. One year, I got up to $2,500 in compensation for software plugins, an Oculus VR set, a few conference tickets and multiple dinners for working on one project. If they do this, they value you in some way. There is that respect and reciprocation I was speaking of. If you work with them again, hopefully, they are consistent with knowing your value to the team and pay you properly.

Game Developers: Here is some info if you haven't found it already. Typically, you might be looking at 5%–20% of your budget cut from the entire budget of the game to be spent. If you're not looking to spend at least that, ask yourself, "What part of quality am I willing to sacrifice from the game for my end users to enjoy? Are they willing to support me in order for me to continue to make games or not?" If you are not going to continue to develop games, then consider that you are only making this game once. Are you going to go all out or are you going to cut corners? No judgement from me. It is your personal call.

Some time ago, Alexander Bruce, developer of Anti-Chamber, mentioned that there was funding for indies and not to make the excuse that you can't pay anyone. Yes, as competitive as it is, it is still worth trying. If you do not try to at least apply for it, you will never know what comes of it.

So, to give a small resolution to the issue, here is my "NPC tip". Look for all avenues of funding outside of the field.

As a developer, I am sure you want to be recognised by each other by the game(s) you create. You WANT people to buy your game. At times, I'm sure you look at professionals who make the game, but those professionals pay at least something to their collaborators. Therefore, you should not expect people to buy your game if you cannot make the effort to offer some sort of fair compensation or trade to a team that is helping you make it.

Xiao'an Li, composer and entrepreneur, gives some insight and advice:

> To begin, this is not to disparage those who take low-paying work. You do what you have to do: we've all been there, and there's nothing to feel ashamed about. Recently, I saw someone post an opportunity in another group that paid 800 bucks per 2–3-minute horror track. I'm going to assume it was a buyout, since it was in a game-focused group. That means that at best, you'd be getting 400 per minute, and at worst, 266.
>
> The standard rate in 1994 for video game music was $1,000 USD. Adjusted for inflation over 2x years, that's around ~$2200 USD now. In 1994, worldwide video game revenues were 20.8 billion. This year, they are 187.7 billion. It has multiplied by more than 9 times. Yes, there are more composers. Yes, getting a working composing setup and education online is a lot easier and cheaper now. But however, it is we got to this point, we're here.
>
> *[However,] if you have the ability to walk away from a low paying gig, you need to use that power to negotiate for more or to educate your clients. It helps you, and it helps everyone else as well.*

In this case, Xiao'an makes the point of not working for free AND not working for nothing! It can be done so, stop working for nothing. Follow the Three Tier Stage System I outlined, and if you're serious about being in the industry, help us rise to the standard. This truly does help all of us. Start putting it into practice, so we can educate the new generation of game developers and become a better industry.

25.10 IMPORTANT SKILLS THAT SHOULD BE LEARNED AND PRACTICED IN GAME AUDIO

So, I have often been asked by students/newcomers what to focus on outside the usual classes if they're interested in creating music and sound design for video games. Most want to know my perspective on skills that can be learned by developing simultaneously in school.

Patience, Research and Communication skills – You can't talk to everyone the same way; stay true to yourself but understand there are different personalities that will not always respond to your communication approach.

I strongly advise developing research skills and practicing social etiquette. I understand that this industry works a lot on trust. You build trust by genuinely getting to know people, not by looking for what they can do for you and also not by being eager to know what you can do for them. People can sense this type of behaviour.

In my opinion, I believe if you want to connect on Facebook, do not send a request without a message, *especially* if you have never met them in person before. I personally think it is good to mention why you want to connect. Hopefully, it is for a genuine reason. Outlining your intentions to connect will give the person some insight into how to proceed. This philosophy holds true for anyone you would like to connect with on LinkedIn.

LinkedIn is seen as a professional platform where people post job and career updates. If you are trying to connect with me, I am thinking that you want to connect professionally and/or tap into my professional network. These professional connections are people with whom I have built a rapport over many years. State your intentions with a message on LinkedIn when you are looking to connect.

Asking for a composition lesson without knowing the type of music the person composes, or Digital Audio Workstation (DAW), will probably not be the best use of your time or the person whom you seek lessons from. Not everyone can be approached the same way or prefers that kind of approach. Do not take most things personally. Just do a little more homework to find your circle in the industry. Sometimes you might have to make that circle yourself.

6/9/2022 (Journal entry on my perspective of the field at this time)

Meeting with some new people in game audio today, I have to say that some of the new generations are smart and extremely skilled people, but their interpersonal skills are very lacklustre. However, at least, they are empathetic but unfortunately, most are still socially awkward. Most forget to follow-up for meetings when they want to speak to someone they admire. Some don't make eye contact and speak so softly that you can't hear them. The reality about this is that most of them will lead things in the near future. I don't sense excitement, passion and confidence. What I do sense is fear, uncertainty and confusion. Everyone is different and has to navigate the space in their own way but if they hope to build a career, the interpersonal skills must level up appropriately. I hope those people get the right help they need and learn, practice and strengthen their communication skills. I think it's important.

As I reflect right now on where I am in my career, I am happy that I don't have to go to every networking event. I am happy that I'm choosing the right people to talk to who get shit done and support my work. I am happy that I'm able to collaborate with like-minded people with the same blue flame and work ethic as me. I no longer have to be in every circle if I don't choose to. I no longer have to have the fear of missing out. Levelling up with my communication and putting the work into myself has helped me grow exponentially. It feels like how it did when I started. I came into the industry *by* myself and I'm going out *like* myself. Who I sought out to be in the beginning is who I am. I will obtain and achieve more before leaving. It's still a marathon but it's slowly turning into an odyssey. For the odyssey, your mind, body and spirit must remain intact at all times in order to make it to the place you love the most and happy.

25.11 THE POWER OF SAYING NO

When you start out to build your worth, say "yes" to most things, then work towards saying "no" to strengthen your value.

The visibility game is taxing. As competitive as people are by nature, social media has made it more difficult. Constantly fighting for attention, sales, work, etc. In order to be heard, you have to cut above the noise and tune into the right frequency.

Some things you get compensated for and other things you don't. At the beginning of 2020, the visibility game started with doing some sample library demos. I reached out to over thirty I wanted to work with and landed a solid two. I had a few others in conversation, but they never panned out. I did three different demos and only one was paid. The trade-off was writing a music demo for a library license.

The second visibility game was game jams. In all, I did Metroidvania jam, Game Boy jam, Ludum Dare 47 and Audio jam.

The third visibility game was guest speaking/panels. This is the biggest and hardest one. Guest speaking isn't for everyone. It takes charisma, courage, discipline and exceptional professionalism to present at a high level. I did a lot of research for many years before entering this arena. In all, by the time 2020 was done, I did 10 presentations, and this was over double than the previous year. I seemed to be able to keep that pace every year.

25.12 WORKING FOR . . . DON'T SAY THE "F" WORD – PERSPECTIVES AND OUTCOMES

I have a personal opinion about this due to my experiences of being taken advantage of, not knowing my own worth and not believing in it the first five years of my career. Even though I was told my work was valuable, at the same time, I was too nice. My mindset has changed, and I believe all trades should be considered for value. If you are approached for work, then you should be compensated.

The universe has a weird way of paying it forward. Your character of charity sometimes blesses you with opportunities and from previous kindness. When I spoke at a prestigious music school, they did not offer any compensation, using the pandemic as a pardon for their thoughtless efforts for my time. However, because I felt it was a good opportunity to be on the panel because I was the only one who did not attend the college at all (in person or virtually), I felt I should do it. Even though my attitude about it wasn't the best, I stayed professional. A year later, they invited me back, sharing that they enjoyed me being on the panel before and would offer me the full treatment of paid expenses/accommodations. I am unsure if I had declined if I would have been invited this year or the other panellists they were considering. I'm unsure if I will fill in a niche for the panel because of my ethnicity. I cannot be concerned about it. I participated to inspire to make a positive impact and to be present.

25.13 "FAKE IT TIL' YOU MAKE IT"

This will only get someone so far and only applies to people who believe in it or believe they "can get over on". You will encounter others who don't support that mentality and go by the motto "If you can't do it 100% then don't". I think one should take caution to possibly use these phrases as tools and not as the be all end all. Be careful with "faking it", it may lead to that self-doubt path I discussed earlier.

25.14 "BE FAITHFUL AND STAY GRATEFUL"

I heard about this phrase from someone named Gabriel while I was at MAGWest 2023. They had a talk about mental health. I thought this phrase was so profound because just like "imposter syndrome", "fake it til' you make it" was another industry catchphrase. Not just in the video game industry but in other industries as well, especially music. Gabe's phrase offers positivity but more importantly truth to face within ourselves.

The other thing that you could be experiencing is psychological insecurities. These are things that you do not feel match the quality of professional peers. The way to combat this is to build on your skill set and practice. Don't practice procrastination. Practice pro-activation. Proper preparedness leads to professional competence and confidence. Once you consistently enact these behaviours, those insecurities will become few and far between and hopefully at some point non-existent.

25.15 FINDING YOUR LANE EARLY

Unfortunately, it seems like a lot of bullshit has been going on in the industry. If you're getting started, figure out your lane now. Figure out where you fit. Figure out the tools that you want to use. Figure out the people that you want to surround yourself with in the circle for things that better your health, not things that diminish it. This is very imperative. Determine the lane that you want to be in. When you try to be in other lanes that you probably and clearly don't align with, I think it's going to be a struggle later on.

Now this is easier said than done. It takes some time but being cognizant about it early and paying attention to the signs and the flags will definitely put you on the right path very quickly. A lot of us don't pay attention to the signs and that's why we feel it's harder to navigate. The universe has a path that is pretty clear for us most of the time, we just have to pay attention. Once you tap in, you find the good people that you need to be around, the ones that will be genuine and support you. Not the fake ones and not the people who check in every once in a while, or every three to five years and there's nothing specifically wrong with those people, they just might not be the folks that belong in your closest circle. I am speaking of the ones that you've had solid conversations with constantly and consistently. That's when you know you're in your lane. Everything else fits into place.

CHAPTER 26

Nobody Cares, Work Smarter Not Harder

As I think about that image, I recall the first time I saw it. Nobody does care. Seldom does anyone ever ask me, "What music have you written lately?" In my many years of relationships, only three women have naturally asked to listen to what music I wrote. "What did you write today? Can I listen to it?", they said. Sometimes my family would not ask. I have to ask if they want to hear it and then they say yes but rarely does anyone ask. My friend Moustafa has asked. My friend Jonathan has asked. A colleague of mine, Kole, has asked. By no means, am I offended but I wonder why they don't ask? However, the majority of old girlfriends, I had to ask for them to share my social media posts. One of them worked in social media. The sad part is she knew the importance of putting the work out there. Another old girlfriend did not ask but had the best feedback for my work when I asked to share it with her. She loved music and she was my muse.

New composers always want their work to be heard and to be critiqued but will rarely ever listen to *your* work first and compliment your work. "Check out my reel! Listen to *my* stuff!" Close industry colleagues who work on music rarely ask if ever. So, it came to a point where I stopped sharing and because of the severe lack of reciprocity, I stopped asking too.

My cognizance deserved a shift in energy and focus. When I read "Nobody cares, work harder" what I comprehended that to be was, "work harder so that somebody cares". But why? Why should I bust my chops for

DOI: 10.1201/9781003422815-26

FIGURE 26.1 Nobody Cares Work Smarter Not Harder

someone to care? As human beings, we are connected to music. So, should we not just care naturally? The awakening exhibited that I am most likely not connected to the people who are naturally interested.

There are other times when you tell people things, and they will make jokes. They may say, "Oh! Hey, how are you doing? Did you win an award yet?" I would reply, "Oh actually I did." and they don't even congratulate me. They don't acknowledge it or anything because they probably were not expecting me to say that I did win, and so, then they just moved on. It appears to feel as though it's nothing to them, and so even with an award, not many seem to deem it successful.

I remember campaigning for awards for some years, and I was getting discouraged because I was hearing from a lot of people saying, "Awards don't really mean anything." Then, I won that award and I received more congratulations than I have gotten birthday wishes. This is a true statement. I wish I could say that wasn't the case, but my point is that people really do care when the right people win. Three times over. What I mean by the "right people" is this. If Naughty Dog wins the award, people typically expect Naughty Dog to win because they have the name. It is one of Sony's first-party studios. They have the money behind the marketing. They have the money to push it all. So, it's like at this point people expect them to win and sweep up in many award categories because they always do. But when the smaller studio or solo person wins, that may still be coming up in the field, that didn't work at Naughty Dog, didn't work on AAA games that had a big marketing budget and push, I think that's what the people were looking for. The people were seeking the hope and the inspiration to say, "Damn they did it. I can do it too."

When I received the award, even my "pre-g" said, "Oh you actually got it?" I was not supported when I won my first industry award. I took a photo with it later and hesitated not to post it. I did not think much of it at the time. I figured I had already been congratulated based on the video announcement. Then, I said, "fuck it" and posted it on social media. I continued to get even more congratulations. It was my highest and most popular post to date. I received warm wishes from people I didn't even know. Over 3k views on LinkedIn, multiple retweets on Twitter X, over 200 likes on Facebook with repeated congratulations from those who wished me before, compliments, warm wishes and some new regards. Afterwards, I thought to myself, I almost did not post this. Then, NYX finally posted the photo that I posted with some compliments as well. Here come more congratulations and likes, even from composers of my childhood, Alberto Gonzalez and David Wise! This was quite humbling and welcoming. I did not hear from the people I sensed were being fake and those who pretended to be my friend when they probably may have envied me. I believe that in this day and age, taking the time to comment on social media shows true effort. To me, it exhibits that "you are worth the time, and I am so moved by it that I will take a moment to celebrate you." Social media likes are nice, and I see them as "kind acknowledgements". I understand that people are "too busy" among other reasons. However, I certainly see the pattern clearly. These experiences gave me a clearer vision on who to build relationships with and how to navigate the industry further. It also outlined who to deal with from afar. In the span of a few months, I grew exponentially faster and smarter.

I was told during the campaign, even by the Fancy Fish development team, that a lot of people don't care about awards. Although that may have been true, I now know and believe that when the right person wins the award, that's what matters. My father didn't call me the first time I posted about the video, because he simply missed the first post, but when the award was in my hand in a photo in the second post and he saw it, he called and congratulated me. From family to random people believe in me and I'll continue to be that inspiration.

However, it fucking sucks! I have to be real. My gosh! I don't mind being the inspiration but what the fuck! I was looking for that inspiration from other people. I cannot help but wonder what if I did not have that tenacious attitude? Would the smaller team or solo person have ever won? When would that have happened? What if it wasn't me with that tenacity and that ambition with that "go get 'em" gusto and everything that makes me who I am? What if that wasn't there? It's deplorable to not see that often.

So, what does it mean to be a multi-award-winning video game composer? You can be a multi-award-winning video game composer, but most people still will not treat you with the respect you have earned. They still ask for free music or for a favour. They will still come up with excuses about why they can't pay you and pay on time. They will still ask you to guest speak for free. Now, I am not sure if it's because I am a minority in the industry or not, but it seems to be apparent with the experience that I have. Currently, I have five awards and three of them are for best soundtrack and some of these event organisations, developers and organisations still do not want to pay me what I am worth. They still do not want to pay me to guest speak and they are still asking for free music. So, again, what does it mean to be a multi-award-winning video game composer as a minority in the field? Does it mean that they don't care? To me, based on the things I just mentioned, it means that I am still not valued at the level I perceive my high value to be. It does not matter how many games I have shipped, how long I have worked in the career, how many guest talks I have presented at the top industry conferences/events/institutions, how many awards I have won, it's not good enough. I wonder if the top-tier AAA composers in Film/TV are approached with the same asks.

Not everyone positions me with this mentality of either aloofness or devaluation. I'm outlining it to bring about the cognizance in hopes that before event organisers or developers consider hiring someone who puts in consistent work and shows a high calibre of professionalism to not disrespect them by requesting their time for free.

My care comes from a genuine place and sometimes I showcase this by sharing my friends' posts to support them. This action is something I don't see too much happening in the game audio community. I stopped caring that people may not like me sharing the success that I see others having.

I like to see others be fully genuine and not follow the "shy etiquette." If they're envious, then they should acknowledge it, try to work through it and make the best effort to learn how to be better. If they stay envious, they most likely will stay in the same position and get passed up by others numerous times. Positivity pushes one to be a better person, and with that, one can become beyond greatness.

In the end, I should care. I am someone. As musicians and composers or any creative, we thrive off feedback. It's how we grow, and we would like for bona fide people to be involved in our lives that truly support the craft that we passionately pour into. The reality is someone does care, and you are the one who must care the most first. Always. If you work harder for yourself, then it builds up the character, confidence, intellect and self-validation to the point where you will just do the work more efficiently and everything else will fall into place.

CHAPTER 27

Step Climbing to Reach the Top of the Flag

In 2021, I remember some new composer getting into game audio asked me, "Why do I do so much guest speaking?" At first, it set me off. I thought to myself, "Isn't it obvious why?" However, I remembered not everyone thinks like me. So, let me explain in proper detail.

I am a video composer who does not look or sound like the majority of other video game composers. That should not matter but it does for the people who play video games and who also do not work in the industry. If the game players discover that their favourite game had people who look like them behind the scenes developing it, then it is most commonly an automatic "like". However, for me, I have to work for it and work hard. I have to prove why I'm worthy to be liked, although my work alone should speak for itself. People's favourite veteran game composers have "Star Power" that they have earned from the 90s, when the job as video game composer was very niche and not as popular to be one. My climb is the "Mario Staircase", and after that, I have to catch the top of the flagpole. I am competing daily against the "Star Power" composers. So, I am not just writing game music, which is a hustle in itself to land decent projects in order to have a career. I am also streaming how I make game music, guest speaking, being on panels, performing my music live, prepping, planning, promoting and releasing game soundtracks by myself, doing music demos for sample libraries in the style of game music, making behind-the-scenes videos for the game projects I scored and promoting all this

DOI: 10.1201/9781003422815-27

FIGURE 27.1 The Physical Super Mario Stairs

work through blogging and vlogging and writing articles. People really do not understand that I have to do about ten different things just to get the acknowledgement off of one thing those veteran game composers did back in the 80s and 90s which is solely write game music. I am literally in almost everything because I need to put myself out there because no one else will do it for me. Not only am I fighting the "Star Power" composers' fan base but I am also trying to gain my own. I have to damn near work myself to bits in order to get noticed.

However, we know that the energy from the "Star Power" eventually runs out and to create 10x of my own energy to keep up with the others' "star power", I become spent as well. I became tired of working so hard. I constantly had to ask for opportunities to be highlighted, learn to be competitive, post infinitely more on social media to be seen, show up to events to be remembered that I exist and do reach out to stay top of mind. I constantly give advice to those who do not do their research/homework, perform at a level just to be considered among those who get bigger opportunities, and constantly reach out to "friendships". I am always the one to initiate. Why? Because as a freelancer, the follow-up comes with the territory.

So, what are the solutions? The best thing to do is to create small goals. One to three follow-ups a day. If there is no response after two follow-ups, then archive it and press on. Filter out those who do not do their research/homework. If they cannot spend the energy/time to do their research, why should you reciprocate the same? Instead of always asking for opportunities, I started creating my own. I record my own content with my own thoughts. I streamed on Twitch my composing process. These are just a couple of solution examples to retain some energy in order to keep climbing until my own star power is reached.

CHAPTER 28

From Rejected to Selected

The Global Game Jam (GGJ) is the world's largest game creation event taking place around the world and is mostly hosted at physical locations. A "game jam" is essentially a "hack-a-thon" focused on game development. Global Game Jam stirs a widespread creative buzz in games, while at the same time exploring the process of development, whether it be programming, iterative design, narrative exploration or any artistic expression. It is all condensed into a 48-hour development cycle.

The GGJ encourages people with all kinds of backgrounds to participate and contribute to this international spread of game development and creativity.

My first Global Game Jam experience wasn't the best. I went to the USC location in Los Angeles because this was the closest location to me. I was very excited as my peers had suggested me to participate. I packed up all of my equipment, a sleeping blanket, a pillow and drove for over an hour to the jam site. I met a few people before the announcement/theme reveal. Things seemed pretty promising. When the disbursement to find a team commenced, I walked around to the few people I met and asked if I could join them. They replied with, "We have someone already." I proceeded to seek out others and was greeted with "No's" and "Our team is full." I began to feel this sense of displacement and disappointment. I drove all the way down to USC to jam and with over 300 attendees on site and there was no place for me. People were already brainstorming and working on their

DOI: 10.1201/9781003422815-28

ideas, and I felt completely left out. I was crushed and so I went home that same night.

In 2018, I decided to give the Global Game Jam a second chance only because it was in a different and much smaller location. I had been to this location before because they had game development meetups. Although this jam facility had a smaller attendance, I was fortunate this time to make it on a team. The experience was much better.

I was happy to have the Global Game Jam experience redeemed.

To take it to the next level, I was asked to be a keynote speaker of Global Game Jam. This was something I could not foresee. I had been doing a lot of guest speaking that year but I took a back seat to slow down and refine the process. Turns out, I was in the top three selections of being a keynote speaker when Tim Cullings asked me. I had never given a keynote before, but I have attended and seen a few. Austin Wintory was the first keynote I had seen at Game Sound Con (2012) and then Marty O' Donnell several years after that.

I proceeded with my keynote research and watched the keynotes from the previous speakers. I have always been a good writer all through college and my prior talks/presentations exhibited the high potency of quality I bring to the table. So, my formula was to:

FIGURE 28.1 GGJ – Theme Reveal

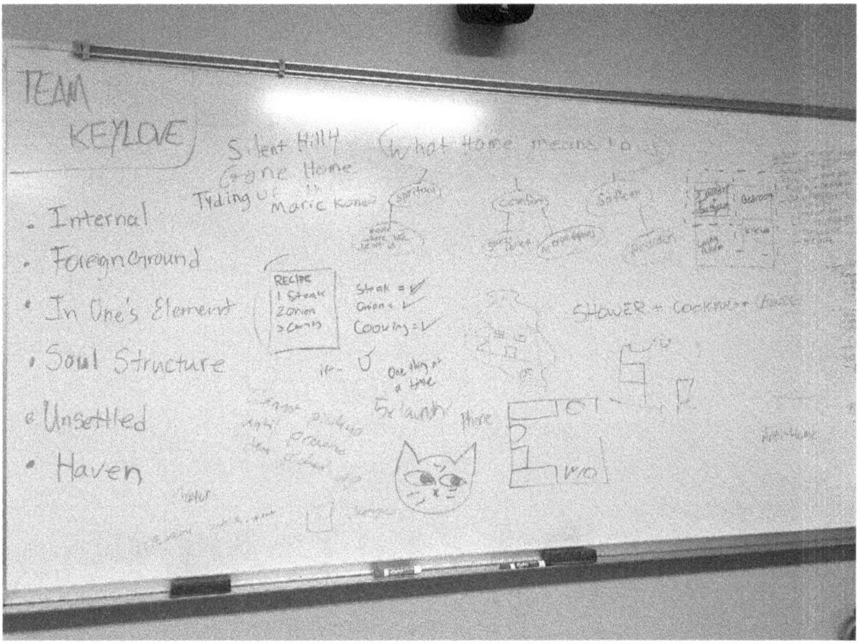

FIGURE 28.2 GGJ – Team Ideas

FIGURE 28.3 GGJ – Composing Station Jam Set-up

FIGURE 28.4 Global Game Jam 2019 Certificate

1. Make a captivating personal story.
2. Share advice that would benefit new and old jammers.
3. Show my personality.
4. Tap into my childhood to reach my audience (i.e. game developers).
5. Research.
6. Make a theme.
7. Have fun.

By this time, I had already watched all but three previous keynote presentations and it took me three days to write mine. My penultimate goal was to make it inspirational for the jammers and to clarify the benefits as well as misconceptions that had been buzzing online about jams in 2020.

It's still an honour to be asked to be a keynote speaker for Global Game Jam. Those that have presented before me are heavy hitters in the field such as Robin Hunicke (Co-Founder and CEO of Funomena) Kyle

FIGURE 28.5 Compliments from the Keynote

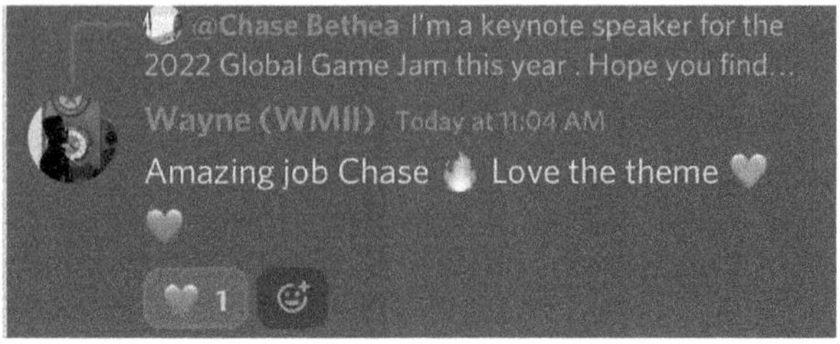

FIGURE 28.6 Compliments from the Keynote

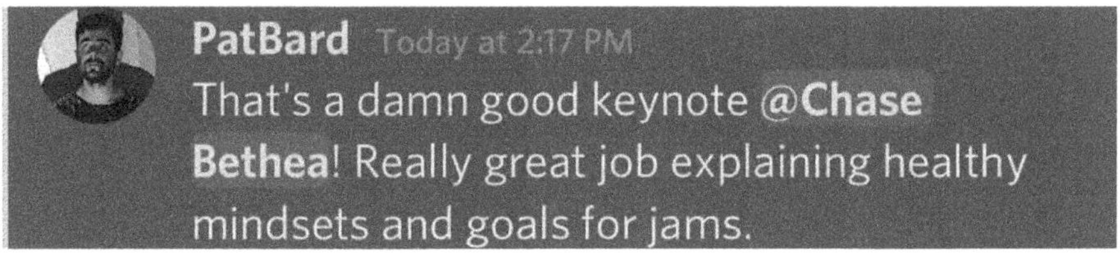

FIGURE 28.7 Compliments from the Keynote

FIGURE 28.8 Global Game Jam Keynote

Gabler, (Game Developer of World of Goo), Keita Takahashi (Developer of Katamari Damacy/We Love Katamari), Jenova Chen (Co-founder and Creative Director of That Game Company – Flow, Flower, Journey, Sky), Guy "Yug" Blomberg (Creator of The GIG, Co-Owner of The Mana Bar) and more.

I believe I am the first keynote speaker to represent the game audio community as a video game composer too. This says a lot, especially since anyone could have been chosen. It resonates deep within me that I was in the top three to be asked/chosen but enough about that. Are you ready to watch it?

CHAPTER 29

Playable Character

One evening, I was in an iASIG meeting with the other steering committee leaders. The previous chair, Kurt Heiden, had mentioned that he was stepping down and that he wanted to nominate someone else to head the organisation. I was slightly swaying and swivelling in my chair while taking a drink when I heard my name mentioned to be nominated. I almost spit out my drink. The other committee leaders had an accord that they wanted me as chair and that I would be a good fit. I told them I'd think about it, and I would have my answer within a day or two. I accepted the position, and I was nervous but honoured to be considered to head this organisation.

The craziest thing I reflect on is my first game audio G.A.N.G. BBQ. This photo has a bit of foreshadowing as I was in the middle of the game audio pioneers, Tommy Tallarico and George Sanger. I will share a little video game audio history. G.A.N.G. (Game Audio Network Guild) and the iASIG (Interactive Audio Special Interest Group) spawned from Project BBQ (an actual BBQ that happened in Texas, where audio software developers and musicians would gather to discuss problems and come up with solutions). Tommy started G.A.N.G. and George started the iASIG (He really jokes about this as the acronym he outlines, "I Actually Started It George"). When I attended what I believe was the last G.A.N.G. BBQ in L.A., I asked to take a photo with George and Tommy. I never would have guessed that ten years in the future, I would be chairman of the iASIG and the universe would choose me to be the next playable character as a leader of one of game audio's legacy organisations.

DOI: 10.1201/9781003422815-29

FIGURE 29.1 Tommy Tallarico, Chase Bethea and George Sanger

May 27, 2022, it had been a week since I've was nominated and voted in as chairman of the Interactive Audio Special Interest Group. It was quite overwhelming catching up with steering committee leaders, previous chairs, founders/pioneers and new potential members but every time I talked to one of those people, I felt like I levelled up. It was like learning the game more and more and I believed that I was getting better at it. I started to feel my influence and saw my opportunities more abundantly. I also began to see the potential others saw in me. The excitement propelled me to make moves with finesse and precision.

One of my goals as chair was to bridge the gap and demystify indie developers working with game audio people. My steps to achieve the goal were 1. Bring game designers together with game audio professionals and educators. 2. Reach out to game companies and share the initiative and ask if they want to be involved. 3. Make a summit that would attract fresh intellectual minds to solve the new era of audio media problems similar to Project BBQ.

My other main initiative was to increase the awareness of the Interactive Audio Special Interest Group. I knew about the legacy of the iASIG but by the time I got to be chair, many new game audio newcomers were unfamiliar, and this was so tragic to me. It was shocking that an organisation that has been around since 1994 did not carry the same recognition as it did in the 90s, 2000s and possibly the 2010s. The game audio community had "deer in headlights faces" whenever I mentioned the iASIG. It was so sad. An industry that set the precedent of game audio workflow solutions and standards for game audio education became somewhat of a fairy tale.

iASIG pioneered and shaped the game audio workflows as we know it from MIDI in games, to work efficiently in mobile. I tried to establish working groups and a new copacetic workflow for VR/AR/MR by talking to Sony and working with their Tempest engine (PS5 Audio Engine) and Steam Audio.

While I was chair, I advocated organising all audio middleware companies to create and finalise the iXMF. This concept started before I was a committee leader but was meant for middleware files to work seamlessly with each other which would have been revolutionary. Just as MIDI works within many DAWs, this iXMF file would work between Wwise, ELIAS, FMOD, Fabric, CRIWARE, Miles Sound System, Krill Audio and more.

Other goal initiatives of mine were having a solid and active steering committee to facilitate and enact tasked responsibilities. Engage the community and keep them motivated by doing panels and giving presentations. Finding and maintaining consistent help and recruiting people who have time and interest. Partner and engage with sponsors. Create compelling content that people want to hear and pull in the IGDA for more resources.

There were a few times, I did not feel like I was the iASIG chair. Kyle Johnson said,

> If you like working on wood and you're a wood maker but your day job is a trash carrier, keep working on the wood even though your day job is different. Enjoy the passion that you have. Don't look at you as being the trash carrier, look at it as being the wood maker.

I found this to be profound and sound advice. My passion was to get the organisation back on its feet again, and with Kyle's great analogy, I found the energy within to do that as long as I could.

As any organisation, it has its challenges and sometimes those challenges have to be worked out without being present, so in 2023 I stepped down. I learned a lot, such as not liking to be a "cat wrangler". This means constantly being on the heels of someone to remind them to get things done. However, I am thankful for the support of Steve Horowitz, the previous chair, Kurt Heiden, and the committee leaders at the time for their faith in my leadership. I'm a self-starter, proactive and an initiator. It does not take a lot to get me going once I am focused, and I reach those goals. In addition, I learned for tasks to be completed, the mindset of the team, as well as the work ethic has to match yours. If not, plans will not be enacted or completed.

I do hope that the iASIG can get back to where it was in previous years. Maybe I will return as chair someday after I accomplish my other goals. It was an honour to be part of the legacy and make an imprint in the field of game audio as I did.

CHAPTER 30

Multiplayer – The Dream Team

During one of my many frustration stages, I finally found an example of what my brand should look like when it comes to professionalism. I was asking myself, why haven't I found an example before and why aren't the people around me pointing me in the right direction? As I cogitated, I discerned that I have to change the strategy of understanding and that I need to attract people who could brainstorm better than me. I thought I was already around those people, but what I identified was a lot of supporters. This was good, however, I needed and wanted creative problem-solvers that fire up and idea the way I do. I re-alchemised my energy to detract leeches and lazy collaborators. I needed and wanted people that are passionate, forward-thinking and thought at a rapid pace. So, I began paying closer attention to the ones I crossed paths with or who crossed paths with me.

Here's a couple things that I did want when I decided on my career. I have always heard of teams. Composer teams. And ten years into my career, I thought I would have that team. About three to four years into my career, I searched for an orchestrator. Not understanding the amount of work, and how much it actually cost, especially once I reached the professional level of having a union orchestrator. Now, I know. By my eighth to ninth year, I felt I had earned a promotion team, agent and a manager. I reached out to agencies in Los Angeles and even in Europe. I took angles such as sending articles I had written about "composer tiers" to agents to

DOI: 10.1201/9781003422815-30

try to pique their attention but to no avail. I never found a team or at least someone that could consistently help me for at least a year. I always had someone who was intermittent or only helped for two weeks or maybe a month. Nothing long term. I also went through a myriad of mixing engineers and mastering engineers. Some of them were mentors. Some of them are close friends who worked in the industry. Every time I thought I would be comfortable with one that would be consistent, they let me down or they rushed through my work. I'm grateful for the help that I did get because at eventide they made time for me even if it wasn't on my schedule.

As I still struggle to find a consistent team that I can rely on to help me reach the next level in my career, I find myself wavering in patience and feeling more spent.

What it meant to be added to the composing module on Tidal. When Tidal asked me to be part of their curated playlist, I was shocked. At first, the Director of Marketing followed me on Twitter, and then, to my surprise, within a few days, I received an email. She offered to update my bio and photo. When I saw my picture on the page alongside the other composers that I have looked up to and industry colleagues, it did something to my mind. It finally made me feel that I was considered a top-tier video game composer.

A lot of people don't know about Tidal, but I recognise it as one of the upper streaming platforms, considering it was designed by top artists in the music industry, such as Jay Z, Taylor Swift and Beyoncé. So, even though a lot of people listen to music on Spotify, Spotify never reached out to me to do a curated playlist of video game music. Tidal did.

I have been considered among the top-tier composers before on Something Else Music Works when I was only three to four years into my career and that gave me a lot of hope. However, being on Tidal next to all the other composers gave me the confidence and propelled my mindset forward to walk with more musical prowess.

Before I was asked to do this, my own creation playlist, I saw the other colleagues in the industry had posted about it and early in the year, I didn't know how they got it, and frankly, I was going through so much in my life, I didn't care to figure out how. I was genuinely happy for them, and all I could think was maybe one day it would be me. It was a small thought. I was mostly elated to receiving that email and euphoric to be considered and added to the composer module page.

"I don't mind if I don't beat the game, I just want to keep playing" (this is in relation to not figuring out how to find the magic formula in all aspects of being successful in game audio).

In this industry, you typically do not do things by yourself. It takes a team or a village. In my case, I have many people who have helped shape my career to what it is today. These are the thank you to those who have remained consistent with their help in my life which in turn shaped my career. You helped this multiplayer experience become a little more manageable in completing the mission.

CHAPTER 31

Parental Influence

In the many interviews that I have done in the past decade, dozens of times I have been asked about my inspiration. When this question is asked of me, I normally respond with composers that I have heard from my childhood to adulthood. On the Games X Music Podcast, when Tom Quillfeldt interviewed me, I mentioned actors being the new influence in the latter part of my career due to their longevity. I do not see actors for a while and they resurface. Actors continuously show up. The majority of A-list actors are still trying to keep their career going. I am not sure what their personal lives are like, but you at least see them in a few films in one year and you see them again in a couple of years. Some time passes, you have not seen them in a while and then they appear in movies again. If they can navigate longevity, I can do it too.

My father is the one who told me very early in my career to remember who I am in this industry and that I'm a minority. This was so that I remained cognizant of any prejudice, microaggressions or career oppressions that I might experience. Let me say that I'm glad he did tell me as those things eventually did betide and when they did, I wasn't shocked.

In my early years, my father bought me an Alto Saxophone. Although I can't recall why I got the Saxophone, I know that I got to choose it. It's through this instrument that I was able to learn how to transcribe and write my own music.

My father introduced me to the PlayStation, and we played *Tomb Raider* (1996) and *Tekken 2*. I remember being at the mall and helping my dad choose between buying *Tomb Raider* and a different game and

DOI: 10.1201/9781003422815-31

FIGURE 31.1 Chase Bethea – Grade 5

I had the influence to get him to buy *Tomb Raider*. I am very glad I did. The two games I played the most were *Resident Evil* and *Tekken 2*, where I beat him 13 times with the character, Law, as he played the character, Lei Wu Long, the cop. He liked the cop character because at the time he was a police officer himself. After beating him so many times, he never played *Tekken 2* again. He was pretty upset and that's valid.

He also bought me my first Sega Genesis. I had wanted this console for years since my best friend (who I consider to be more of a brother), Efosa, had one that I would sometimes get to play. He got a good deal at Hollywood Video, and they were liquidating their games. The PlayStation and N64 were increasingly becoming more popular at this time. I did not care. I got to own and play *Pit Fighter, Pitfall The Mayan Adventure, Earthworm Jim, Outrunners, Pebble Beach Golf Links, Mega Turrican, The Lion King, Sonic 2, Sonic Spinball, Mortal Kombat II, Street Fighter, NBA Jam, Madden 96, NFL Quarterback Club 96, Shining Force, Shining in the Darkness, Comix Zone, WWF Royal Rumble, Desert Strike, Jungle Strike, Taz-Mania, Streets of Rage, Barkley Shut Up and Jam, F15 Strike Eagle II, Ecco the Dolphin, Ecco The Tides of Time* and *Genesis 6-Pak*. This is where I discovered one of my beloved games, which I always mention in podcast interviews, *Beyond Oasis*. The alto saxophone, PlayStation and Sega Genesis influence comes through him.

My grandma is the reason gaming is in my life. She supported my gaming interest since my cousin visited from Barbados with a Game Boy playing *Donkey Kong '94*. She bought my first Game Boy and some games and also bought my first N64 and some games for it too. However, as I mentioned before, I discovered the Intellivision because my grandma had it under the bed in a spare bedroom. This discovery broadened my world of gaming even more. Thinking about it now, I get excited for the first time connecting the system as a 7-year-old and playing *DragonFire*. Grandma encouraged my gaming because she knew it was an escape for me, and it made me happy. I'm super thankful for her doing the best she could buy me those consoles. They have truly created some of the happiest memories.

My great-grandmother, Laurie, told me at a very early age to always stay humble. She said, "No matter how big (in terms of success) you get or how much money you make, stay humble, Chase." For some reason, this advice stuck to me, even though I was hearing it between the ages of 5 and 7, I have to say that it has paid off. At times, when my ego has gotten big, my self-awareness kicks in and I remember my great-grandmother's voice, "Stay humble." I check myself and tuck my ego in, and when I have done this, a lot more opportunities have opened up for me in life.

Working in games for the past decade, I have only met a few people who have had and maintain the mindset of humility. I deeply commend them, and as we have crossed paths, kind has recognised kind. Unfortunately, the field is filled with self-inflated egos, and it makes it incredibly difficult to manoeuvre. If you're not kissing ass, you don't progress as much as I have seen others do. However, the massive egos can push people away very quickly and I have seen careers dissipate due to the inflation of it becoming too much. The field is small and word travels faster than sound or the speed of light. Well, maybe not that fast but you would be surprised how quickly a reputation is tarnished if someone becomes too big of an asshole for too long. For me, humility is an innate characteristic. I am cognizant that at any moment things can be worse (because they have happened before), so, while I have more fortunate moments, I remain grateful and always will. Although my great-grandmother did not express in detail why to stay humble, I still became aware on my own by learning from tough life experiences. Thankfully, by her saying those words to me, her influence has served me well in my career field.

My mum raised me to think differently, to watch, listen and learn. To learn from her mistakes. Her work ethic is unparalleled from being a full-time creative herself and working multiple day jobs. She taught me how to be professional and have a strong work ethic as well as be a man of my word. Most importantly, she taught me how to take responsibility and accountability. Through all these lessons, I chose to take from them and incorporate them into my life and career. The bar was set high in terms of decorum, diplomacy and professionalism when I entered the field, and I thought that others would operate on the same level. However, over time, I had discerned and accepted that was not the case and so I had to adapt and pivot accordingly.

Setting the standards of manners, strong mindsets of willpower and the belief of belonging. It is because of her that I learned how to establish my signature sound 20 years ago. She was the first to indirectly clue me in on creating dynamic music as she would always complain that music in the games I was playing in adolescence was very repetitive.

In addition, my mum taught me how to take constructive criticism as she would be brutally honest with my earliest work that I made years before I started my career in games. I grew tough skin quickly and this allows me to be very flexible when working with development teams when it comes to possible revisions. This experience also taught me to write better and quicker. This influence pushed my creativity in the most positive way as I was always encouraged to keep trying, and when I did write something that she liked, she would dance and/or praise the work.

My mum, Cheridah, is a triple, if not a quad-threat. An award-winning actress, singer, dancer and businesswoman. She is exceptionally talented. From an early age, I had been around music here. She performed many theatre shows that are known on Broadway, acted in Hollywood films such as "Ferris Bueller's Day Off", "Next Friday" and "The Nutty Professor" and recorded award-winning audiobooks as well like "The Child Prince". My mum had been singing to me since I was in the womb. She bought me some instruments as a child that I still use today in my video game compositions. It's without a doubt the biggest influence is my mum.

31.1 PITCH SHIFTING

Why did I start taking vocal lessons? I used to take them before with my mum when I was 16 but I quit. Something told me to continue them again in 2021. So, I asked my mum to give me lessons again. I believe I truly learned how to sing better than before. I was mature and could take criticism with more poise. I discovered some other things as well.

The lessons helped with counterpoint. Find the key your song is in. Pick a reference you like with the key. Sing a countermelody over it and that becomes your melody for your piece or countermelody.

Working with singers in more capacity gives me a better understanding of the instrument. When a singer explained their range, it provided me with the information on how to indite for them specifically. I can discern what is too low and especially too high and draft contours that complement their unique voice.

Vocal lessons also helped with pitch intonation with signing on my work. From here, I was able to develop a stronger tone with my voice and ear. It also meant I potentially added another instrument to my arsenal.

"If you listen as much as you wanted to be heard, you would hear how to be listened to." – Mum

Ever since I was young, Mum always said to me, "Watch, listen and learn". I can remember her saying that to me since I was in second grade. I suppose that is why I can pick up patterns in music and in people. However, by listening, I noticed that when I wrote music, most of them were not listening. They did not understand what I was making. They criticised my work and said I did not have melodies, when I did. They were not listening. They did not understand the chord progressions I was doing, when jazz was doing the same. They did not listen. It was something about what I did that didn't make sense to them. I listened to what they were doing, and

I understood. However, they could not because I didn't sound like every other Hollywood media composer, and so, I was, well frankly, ignored. What this taught me was that I never had to try to constantly cut above the noise. People who were interested would tune into the right frequency. I just had to write what was comfortable and that made me happy.

I am most grateful for the inculation my mum did with how to carry myself professionally and how to navigate the industry. In addition, I am thankful that I understood what to take from those teachings and implement them as well.

CHAPTER 32

Load Save

It's funny. We see this phrase, "what I wish someone told me when I started." As I'm writing this, I'm thinking to myself, there's a lot of that.

I wish someone would've told me within the first five years of my career that my music is really good, but I just need better resources to make it sound competitive (i.e. higher-end sample libraries, and money for an orchestra/orchestrator). Also, my music production wasn't up to par in order to get the bigger gigs and that I need to hire a mixing engineer or take music production classes.

I wish someone would've told me that when you're starting out and you don't have a lot of money that you didn't need to have ($700–$1000) in order to buy a GDC (the Game Developers Conference) pass. You could just book a ticket, find a place to stay and just be around people and the conference to meet up with people in the area/parties.

I wish someone would've told me that you need to take a business class or a finance class in college. If you decide that you're going to be a freelancer/entrepreneur, especially in video game audio. This is necessary in order to survive in an expensive metropolitan municipality.

I wish someone would've told me that 3D games are very expensive and hard for those who are not trained or experienced in working at a game studio to know how to fund and maintain the game development process in order to ship one. This will be a "portfolio limiter" as getting onto those projects is rare. If the game never ships at a stable, playable build, it may be hard to qualify it as a credit to leverage future work.

DOI: 10.1201/9781003422815-32

I wish that someone would've told me that not everyone's going to be your friend. There are people who aren't going to like you and people whom you aren't going to like either. This is life in general, but I mention this because that catchphrase that many people say in the industry is "People want to work with their friends." So, I think many people have this perception that they *need* to make and sometimes force friendships in order to get work or game credits. I believe this isn't a good or safe mentality to sustain. Instead, meeting people with zero expectations and if something comes from it, it will be less stressful and more of a mental relief.

I wish that someone would've told me that sometimes this industry is like high school and that there are "cliques". In addition, there is an imbalance of favouritism, nepotism and you have to learn to deal with that until you find your path, make your own squad, discover your own tribe or search for your own supporters that genuinely want to see you succeed. It's good to remain balanced. Don't stay in one group. Mix into others. Learn about the people in them. I have found that staying in one group limits your perspective about this massive field. With the ability to manoeuvre between multiple groups, you should be able to remain in balance with the mindsets that you encounter as long as you are optimistic. This should also offer the advantage of helping others with solutions as you'll be able to hear about more problems.

If you've played *The Legend of Zelda: Majora's Mask* on N64 or DS, you may recall that Link helps many people in the town over the course of three days. Luckily for you, you have more than three days, but the point is that Link roams around town talking to many to solve problems. Of course, this is part of the story mechanic but the principle outside of the game is just as effective. Art imitates life after all.

There also seems to be a false preconception for beginning composers that going to GDC is going to get you a gig. However, it sometimes is not going to bring you a gig – not directly. You're hopefully there to foster industry relationships in a genuine manner. When your network reaches a critical mass and your timing coincides with a need (remember, game development cycles are extremely long), that's when a gig may come to you.

I wish that someone would've reminded me that it is easier to be yourself rather than trying to fit in. So, if you stand out, you stand for a better reason that hopefully will be recognised later. I think it's a hell of a lot easier to naturally stand out than to try to fit in somewhere you do not belong.

I operated with this mindset in high school but for some reason when entering the video game field (a.k.a. "the bigger high school"), I somehow forgot. I keep it at the forefront of my mind now.

I wish that someone would've told me to find out who is serious and who is not. You may come to discover that when you're hustling early in the game that you want a response from everyone. In the first maybe five to eight years, this mentality may be perceived as good . . . or is it? The tip is you have to manoeuvre fast. The people who do not respond have patterns. People who want to work with you will most likely respond. People who look in your face at GDC and other game conferences and tell you, "that they want to collaborate", send a follow-up and then you wait two weeks for a response and send another follow-up and repeat the process. The majority of the time, this gets you nowhere and these people are not serious about working with you. They may have been leading you on. The other cases may be where something tragic has occurred in their life or they got busy and may have forgotten and may not see you as a priority. However, they may be incapable of taking two minutes to briefly write, "Hey I got this email, and I am currently inundated. I'll do my best to get back to you soon." It happens to the best of us. Unfortunately, I have been on the exhausting follow-up side of this more often than I would like to count.

The best mentality solution I can share is to try not to fault them for it but continue to move. A phrase that is often said is "Do not take it personally." Easier said than done. It takes a lot of mental practice and discipline to do. Something I did when these scenarios transpired was I took several deep breaths in and out. Then, I said these words out loud, "I will not take it personally." This strengthened my mental stamina.

Secondly, you have to keep moving upwards. After three follow-up emails, keep it pushing like Lara Croft moving those big ass bricks in *Tomb Raider* (1996). Do not do what I did. In my fourth year of the field, I emailed a developer for nine months and never got a response. I compared this to when I reached out to an AAA composer who I did not think I would ever get a response from and eventually I did after emailing him for a year. I had already met the developer and the composer in person, so both emails were not cold ones. They told me to reach out. So, when I was trying to connect with the developer, I thought if I was consistent, they would respond. However, what I did not know was that I should not be comparing it to the situation. I should be comparing their personalities. So, I set a limit and said, "Okay the first email will most likely be missed. I will send a second and third." I stretched the outreach timeline to once a month or every two months. This also came down to the project I was seeking and how specific I was to whom I wished to connect with. This is something I wish I knew a little sooner in my career rather than a decade in.

I wish someone had told me that some people want you to do good, but they don't want you to do better than them. When people can't process your success, they don't see it happening for themselves or it's too good to be true in their eyes of reality, that's when you receive the side remarks, the "change up" and the envy. Those people may talk to you less than they did before. They may not like or comment or reshare on your posts as much. Here's the truth and what I wish someone had told me at the start of my career. It's okay. What is mine will be for me. No one or nothing can or will stop it. Their insecurities have nothing to do with me. I'm grateful that I am not a hater. I love seeing others shine, do well and I'm one of the most genuine and consistent people who showcase it. How can I continue to receive good luck and fortune if I'm hating someone else? I can't. So, I don't. Greatness awaits but can only be enacted from within.

Although these are things I wish I could load a save file on and retry, I am thankful to learn from the lessons and retain the experience. This can now be a new save point that I can load from a decade from now as I carry the loot of applied knowledge here forward.

CHAPTER 33

Infinite Mana

> I had to learn to seek to work with those who want to *work with me, not work against me.*

There was a time when I was stuck on why people around me are not capable of pointing me in the right direction. So, I decided to address how to change the strategy of understanding and attract people who can brainstorm better. I thought I was around those people, and I have great supporters, but I needed brainstormers. I need people who fire up on the ideas the way that I do and I need to not attract leeches and not attract lazy collaborators. I need to attract people who are forward-thinking, passionate and create a rapid way of thinking. So, I did not know how I was necessarily going to begin that, but I figured I would start by seeking that and paying closer attention with a sharper eye.

33.1 KEEPING A PART-TIME JOB FOR CONSISTENT INCOME

It seems to be a facade that if you are a freelancer, you can work full-time in game audio. The running ideology and mentality is that "No one has money" and "No one can pay you". Well, there are people who can pay you. They are quality people who value work and ethics and you need to find them. It might take some time but do not give up and continue to search for them. The ones that do not value you, just move on. You will be wasting your energy and time. Do not try to build relationships with those people because the mentalities do not match. It is something that you need to be able to understand from the beginning. Let them deal with

DOI: 10.1201/9781003422815-33

themselves and run themselves into stress and overworking practice. The people who value you will definitely pay you right off the top. You will not have to ask often or if ever.

Try to set yourself some financial freedom. They say, "Don't quit your day job" but I feel like this is "killing the dream". It is a harsh reality, and we probably need to hear that. However, what I have come to realise is a puzzle piece to just find a part-time job that you are also passionate about, that you could love and that you can undergo for a long time in the most positive way. It is healthy. The part-time job gave me the financial freedom to free my mind creatively. I was able to hire studio or live musicians and pay them for their work, hire an orchestra, and save up for plug-ins and/or equipment. Whatever I wanted, it definitely liberated me because I did not rely on companies to pay for those resources. If you're freelancing, do not rely on these companies and small team developers to pay your bills. You are responsible for that and having a part-time job definitely helps out with everything creatively. You will find in the long term that you will love the creative process and the field overall a little bit more. In addition, more sustainability will become possible too. I do believe in this a lot, and you would not be the only person who has done it. There are many of who we consider to be "the greats" and a lot of other people, who I believe are now at the top who are not talking about it, but they definitely have walked this path before. I do not feel those at the top who have been through this have not been transpicuous enough, but I figured it out and I believe it is good to share.

We all have the same allotted time in a day. It is what we do with it and how we direct our energy that determines how much progress we are able to achieve in that span of time.

CHAPTER 34

Choose Your Endgame

When I came home from GDC one year, I left my suitcase by the door. Something was waiting for me in the mailbox that I really wanted to reach but the suitcase was in the way. Even though I thought multiple times, I will just pull out a couple of clothes and do a couple of things. I wanted to initially do laundry and then get to the item that was in the mailbox. But then I thought, what if I just unpacked the suitcase one by one and that way it'll eliminate what's in the suitcase and clear the pathway. Then, I can unlock the door and reach what is in the mailbox. The analogy for this is that sometimes things are in our way and there is a lot to unpack. We have to put things aside, put them away and finish them properly before we can reach what we want to get to. Although this exercise was physical, it was a nice mental activity to attribute to the work that we do in this field. There are sometimes impediments, and we do not put them away properly and it still becomes an obstruction because we may trip over it or we may ignore it when we become too tired, procrastinate or give up. However, the key here is consistency and discipline. With this, you can achieve what you want to get to.

As you grow older in this field, hold more accolades on your shoulder, and they offer you exposure, it becomes harder to keep your composure when you're a multi-award-winning composer, keynote speaker and nationwide published author. So, the ambition of soldiers gets bolder.

As you approach the endgame, there are some imperative questions to ask yourself.

DOI: 10.1201/9781003422815-34

FIGURE 34.1 The Long Road

Is the industry discipline that I am pursuing sustainable? My previous mentor, Ken, warned me when I was at CSUN (California State University, Northridge) that it was not sustainable and he worked on two AAA games at the time. So, if you are looking to have a family or you already have a family, you should ask yourself this question because if you choose to walk it, it will be a peregrination.

I strongly believe it's healthy to have a sustainable job so that you can choose the projects that you want. The field does not show consistent maturity and sustainability. This is just the era we're in. I don't see it ever going back to being a level playing field because there's way too much competition as well as a plethora of distractions happening where you're playing against an algorithm and competition. Those two things are mentally hard to beat. I do suggest, as I've said before, keep doing your own thing, keep staying curious and that leads to your art. Hopefully, by doing this, it will be because you love it. It'll remain your passion. If anything bigger comes of it, that's a bonus stage. *Be* grateful if it betides because I believe it to be very rare.

Other questions to ask yourself are, how passionate am I about this? Am I willing to accept revisions from different client developers that may or may not know what they want, even though penalties are outlined in the contract? If so, how long? Am I willing to receive a lot of rejections? When the rejections occur, they are hard on the brain and burnout will transpire. These specific burnouts will be the result of lack of control and insufficient rewards. The reward does not mean from a financial standpoint. It can come from not getting as much out of the energy as you are putting in and encompasses everything that should be rewarding from it.

More questions to consider. How will I deal with the wins? If you do not take the time to enjoy the process that comes with the hard work, you may find yourself to be unsatisfied. You may be thinking, "Okay, what is the next thing?" This is a dangerous tautological cycle. Stop, pause and celebrate the win.

Reflect and meditate on what you did, and more importantly, why you did it. What should come from this introspection is gratitude. In addition, take a moment to breathe and properly pace yourself into the next day.

Next question. Do I have all the business acumen to get started and/or sustain? A large number of these small developer teams and big AAA companies do not know how to run a business. This is a fact. If you do not know, I highly encourage you to do your homework on the lay-offs that have come to pass in the industry pre-2024 and do some proper inquisition to see the annual trends of these lay-offs as well as the executive bonuses that are ensured before or after the dismissals of employees take place. Do not get caught up in the crossfire. Applied knowledge is power.

Everything has a rhythm, speed, time, pattern, reason and purpose. The best way to navigate is to discern how to adjust and flow with all of them.

So, in summary, what has it been like the past decade? It's been good, it's been interesting and a hard path to consistently walk to say the least. There are so many more adjectives to describe the odyssey as I culminate the experiences of it all. The fact remains that it has been about the consistency, the mentality and the willpower of knowing where you belong and running with it.

FIGURE 34.2 Cheers to the Finish Line

Bibliography

Copland, Aaron. 1988. *What to Listen for in Music*. Signet Book.

Greening, Chris. 2016. "Annual Game Music Awards 2015 – Artists of the Year." *VGMO-Video Game Music Online*. February 14. http://www.vgmonline.net/awards2015artists/.

Li, Xiao'an. n.d. "Fuck You Pay Me." *Fuck You Pay Me*.

Marks, Aaron. 2012. *The Complete Guide to Game Audio: For Composers, Musicians, Sound Designers, Game Developers*. 2nd ed. Independence: CRC Press.

Parnell, Rebecca. 2017. "10 Essential Tips for Game Audio Freelancers." *A Sound Effect*. A Sound Effect. February 13. https://www.asoundeffect.com/10-essential-tips-game-audio-freelancers/.

Sparks, Clinton. 2019. "How to Win Big in the Music Business." *2020 Clinton Sparks*. https://www.amazon.com/How-Win-Big-Music-Business/dp/B08MVCGB7Q.

Index

For Product Safety Concerns and Information please contact our EU
representative GPSR@taylorandfrancis.com
Taylor & Francis Verlag GmbH, Kaufingerstraße 24, 80331 München, Germany

www.ingramcontent.com/pod-product-compliance
Ingram Content Group UK Ltd.
Pitfield, Milton Keynes, MK11 3LW, UK
UKHW022118190926
475702UK00013B/1518
9781032685397